You cannot write about education and think
only of schools.
(Neill, 1936, p 75)

We want some honesty. We want some sticking to the law.
We want them to be clear about what they are doing. We
want them to stop hiding home education because people
might want to do it, and I have heard that very often.
(Alison Sauer to House of Commons Education
Committee, 2012, p Ev 6)

Deep-seated prejudice against home education is
widespread. (Home Education Advisory Service to
House of Commons Education Committee, 2012,
p Ev 40)

Nothing is beautiful or loving or political aside from
underground stems and aerial roots, adventitious growths
and rhizomes. (Deleuze and Guattari, 2004, p 15)

Is there no language with which we, as philosophers, can
say anything insightful about parents and children, other
than the language of rights, duties, authority
and responsibilities?
(Suissa, 2006, p 67)

EDUCATION WITHOUT SCHOOLS

Discovering alternatives

Helen E. Lees

First published in Great Britain in 2014 by

Policy Press
University of Bristol
6th Floor
Howard House
Queen's Avenue
Clifton
Bristol BS8 1SD
UK
Tel +44 (0)117 331 5020
Fax +44 (0)117 331 5367
e-mail pp-info@bristol.ac.uk
www.policypress.co.uk

North American office:
Policy Press
c/o The University of Chicago Press
1427 East 60th Street
Chicago, IL 60637, USA
t: +1 773 702 7700
f: +1 773-702-9756
e:sales@press.uchicago.edu
www.press.uchicago.edu

British Library Cataloguing in Publication Data
A catalogue record for this book is available from the British Library

Library of Congress Cataloging-in-Publication Data
A catalog record for this book has been requested

ISBN 978 1 44730 641 2 hardcover

Cover design by Policy Press
Front cover: istock
Printed and bound in Great Britain by CPI Group (UK) Ltd, Croydon, CR0 4YY
Policy Press uses environmentally responsible print partners.

FSC
www.fsc.org
MIX
Paper from
responsible sources
FSC® C013604

This book is dedic
around the world u
their chilc

Contents

List of abbreviations

BERA	British Educational Research Association
DCSF	Department for Children, Schools and Families
DfE	Department for Education
DfES	Department for Education and Skills
EHE	Elective home education
EWO	Education Welfare Officer
EWS	Education Welfare Service
GHEC	Global Home Education Conference
HEAS	Home Education Advisory Service
HL	Helen Lees
LA	Local authority
MOOC	Massive Online Open Course
SEN	Special Educational Needs

Notes on author

Dr Helen E. Lees is Associate Research Fellow in the Faculty of Education and Theology at York St John University. Her research interests focus on the democratic alternative in and for education. She has published a monograph in 2012: *Silence in Schools*, London: Trentham Press, which looked at the effects for democracy of silence practices in the institution of the school. Other published work and work in progress can be seen on her www.academia.edu profile page. She is founding Editor-in-Chief of the online open access journal *Other Education – the journal of educational alternatives:* www.othereducation.org.

Acknowledgements

I would like to profoundly thank the research participants who feature in what follows for their generous willingness to share with me their experiences. Thanks to all at Policy Press; especially Emily Watt and Isobel Bainton. The following people – amongst others – have helped me with comments on the draft manuscript and/or with useful encouragement for this work: Harriet Pattison, Ian Stronach, Richard Davies, Fiona Nicolson, Alan Thomas, Michael Reiss, and Maurizio Toscano.

This book emerges from the satisfying and enjoyable PhD research journey conducted at the University of Birmingham during 2007–2010; an experience assisted by the School of Education, who also gave me full funding. I was very lucky and grateful to be supported there by Professor Clive Harber and Dr Nick Peim, as main and second supervisor respectively. Apart from the deep respect I feel for their own work – such that I moved from London to Birmingham for the chance to work with Clive, and his writing was my first academic inspiration – I owe these two scholars so much. They validated and encouraged my research interests in educational alternatives and otherwise approaches, from the first contact.

Thanks to Ann and Alex Lees and you Guglielmo, as always, for all that you do.

ONE

Setting the scene

Samantha: 'I think lots of people don't know that it's actually legal to home school. They think going to school is something a child has to do.
Helen Lees (HL): Do you think that's bad?
Samantha: *Yer!!*

Introduction

This is a book for educational academics and policy makers. But it is also a book for all educationists, especially teachers and parents. For both audiences it offers a double narrative. On the one hand it speaks about education and educational studies, on the other it relates directly to people's experiences about how education affects lives and educational decisions. Both narratives are important and intertwined for both groups. I would even say that they can bring people together.

I hope to broaden the hegemonic concept of education most of us currently work with, impacting upon it for change. This is work for the two audiences mentioned above. The work is for education to be a more dialogic and flexible, responsive concept, held between the rights, responsibilities and expertise of parents, teachers, academics and policy makers.

Whilst this is a big ambition, it is served by the data of the study to which this book connects. This data is from a small-scale study with significant and surprising ramifications. What is important in what I say comes directly from what people have told me. The voices of the research participants are crucial and central to this book's presentation. So, I am telling an educational story from research. But through recourse to this story, some theoretical points are also made in sociological, political, philosophical terms and contexts about how education functions.

The book offers:

- New empirical evidence showing that, for adults, contemporary mainstream schooling is their main educational concept. Schooling means education and education means schooling.
- Discussion of how adults do not have to see education as schooling. Indeed, the data shows that they actively wish to know it as something else also, encompassing a broader universe of different worlds of practice and theory.
- Consideration of positive information provision about educational options beyond school choice. Many adults, as taxpayers, want and seek to discover, from official state providers, information about educational difference beyond mainstream state schooling. They want this in clear conceptual terms that can be utilised as everyday knowledge, whether they are parents or not.
- A way forward so that a broader concept of education can be made politically and socially feasible because of democratically free discovery of alternative pathways.

By offering a structural reorientation of our present understanding of education, whether as schooling or otherwise, the book also provides and is supported by:

- Empirical evidence that discovering alternative educational pathways is profoundly life changing and therefore of broad significance for educational studies as an academic activity.
- Discussion of what education means if it can have such significance that finding new ways of doing it may affect one's outlook on life, social and political behaviour and even beliefs.
- A new outlook from educational studies challenging policy makers and educationists to accept responsibility for a widely held broader working concept of education. This would include integrating alternative practices and theories as *equal* players in education, which is currently hegemonically defined and predetermined as schooling.

So one story is practical: about the how, why and what-to-do-about of discovery of the possibility of education without schools in a democracy. The other: an existential theme of the impact of education without schools on how adults conduct their social and personal responsibilities and how they see their place in the world as 'citizens' and educators of others.

By presenting empirical evidence from the research study mentioned above, conducted on the discovery of alternative educational pathways by adults – and especially parents – the task is developed within the context of current developments in educational studies. This is done particularly where they relate to the idea of education as needing and even seeking alternative viewpoints.

The supporting study

The study underpinning the presentations, analysis and conclusions of this book was conducted between 2009–2010, in England. Further particulars about this study, including details of its methodology, can be found in the Appendix. A diverse range of adults were interviewed in depth about the moment they discovered that an alternative to mainstream schooling was possible. Also, using a street-survey method, adults who were encountered by the researcher on the street or on public transport were asked if they knew that education without schools was possible and their answers were noted.

The interviews looked at the moment of discovery. It was treated as an important event and showed a sudden shift in perspective by the interviewee as it occurred. This analysis came about because the data was in line with Kuhnian paradigm shifts involving anomaly, crisis and resolution via revelation (Kuhn, 1962). The aim of asking about these moments was to first identify if they existed and, if so, in what manner. Second it was to consider the impact of discovery on the participants and ask about the effects and implications of finding out that 'compulsory' mainstream schooling was not the only educational option in England for them.

Background to the study

In England – as elsewhere in the UK,[1] with England used as a case study for wider implications which also hold in many other countries around the world – the majority of children go to a state connected school. The landscape of schooling in England has changed since 2010 when the study was carried out, with the subsequent election of a Coalition government. This has brought in a reconfigured educational landscape when it comes to schooling. Academies now proliferate and free schools, studio schools and university technical colleges emerge. Maybe eventually other kinds of schools will also be possible, especially for the secondary school age range. It is a situation where no new school can, since 2011, be established without it being either a free school or an academy because:

> ... the Education Act 2011 states: 'If a local authority in England thinks a new school needs to be established in their area, they must seek proposals for the establishment of an academy.' Under the government's guidelines, councils can also establish free schools. (Lloyd, 2012)

This means that the concept of a hegemonic 'national' state-run school system is being deconstructed or, at least, changed. What this signifies for English education is yet to be fully determined. In-depth discussion of this factor – for instance, whether these developments offer 'difference' or not – is outside the remit of this book.

However, an increasing (potential) diversity of educational provision in England links strongly to the issues that this book discusses of diversity, choice, parental options and information, as well as the effect of educational diversity on the lives and learning of young people. My focus is to look beyond the school and therefore whether academies and free schools currently genuinely offer diversity is not the concern. I am also looking, as will be seen in chapters to come, beyond the state. It need not be the case that the state is 'overlooked', but as I show, sometimes people have no other option but to find their own solutions because the state is not taking appropriate action, in line with its own recommendations, agreements and laws.

The aim of the book is to provide a radical perspective on diversity. The very idea of the school is challenged. It presents a way to understand education for young people that need not, and often does not, include the school. The context then is English education as an arena that may or may not include school attendance. England serves in this way as a case study for other countries of what can happen and also what is possible. The law in England allows for education without schools, but the concept and the information to support the concept is lacking amongst the general population. It is also, surprisingly, very weak as a concept amongst many academics and policy makers. How, why, the effects of this and how to deal with education without schools in the context of an educational system that functions through schooling is the remit of this book.

The Kuhnian aspect requires also background explanation. Why is the idea of a gestalt switch moment so important to education without schools? Above I have hinted at a hegemonic schooling paradigm that dominates signification of what we mean by the word 'education'. When it comes to adults understanding education in the everyday, and often this means *for* their children, it is certainly true, as I outline later, that most adults think 'school', when the word 'education' is mentioned.

The significance of such a situation is profound for the discovery of alternative pathways. It means that realising that education is not schooling is an *event* in the life of an adult. It is a mental event with practical consequences. At this moment adults have made a discovery enabling them to change their own life and the life of their family. The pattern of this occurrence happens in a similar way to patterns of discovery in the natural sciences. This is discussed in more detail from a theoretical point of view in Chapter Four, and Chapter Five shows what happens, via presentation of the empirical interview 'discovery moment' data.

Regarding the concept of education, confusion can come about for those who are living in a world where there is a mismatch between the rhetoric and the reality of schooling. Broadly, the idea is that education offers self-development through the acquisition of knowledge, answering problems created by ignorance. This helps people to 'get along' (interpersonally and with socio-economic success) as common citizens. Ideally, *schooling* will deliver this widely held promise to parents for their children; parents are aware of this promise and this 'contract'. The following comment illustrates this idea:

> ... of course, most parents would assume, I would have thought quite properly, that their responsibility is to send their children to school during schooling age. (Neil Carmichael MP, House of Commons Education Committee, 2012, p Ev 2)

But for some individuals schooling fails to realise and deliver on the promise: the assumed responsibility of parents to send their children to school then becomes instead a responsibility to *remove* them from or *avoid* schooling for a variety of reasons. School attendance seems like a bad idea in the light of this responsibility. It is not helping and may even be harming. Harm from schooling is unfortunately common and globally widespread, including significant problems seen in the UK (see Glover et al, 2000; Osler, 2006; Harber, 2009b; Harber and Mncube, 2013; Lees, 2013b). Its capacity to do harm is widely underestimated in favour of believing blindly in the promise, rather than facing up to a less attractive and rather difficult, often failing, reality.

People who are confused over the supposed 'goodness' of education seek for answers to a mismatch; they retain belief in education but lose faith in schooling. So, they search for alternatives to schooling as a solution to difficult situations caused by or to do with schools. In England, at least, a viable and legal solution is to home educate.

Another option is to turn towards a different form of educational philosophy instead of that supporting most mainstream provision. This is largely found in private schools, such as those offering radical democratic schooling, where children choose what to learn, when and often even how. Two such schools exist in England: Sands School in Devon and Summerhill School in Suffolk (see Gribble, 2001). Other kinds of alternative provision such as Montessori or Steiner schools are limited in number, intake provision and by geographical location (see Carnie, 2003). Some free schools are now beginning to emerge, and these may seek to take an alternative approach as their underpinning educational rationale.

However, the vast majority of those seeking 'alternatives' will search for, and can find, elective home education practice. The number of home educators in England is somewhere between 20,000 and thousands beyond that.[2] Because home educators (in the UK) do not need to compulsorily register their practice with a local authority if a child has never attended nursery or school, numbers are always only 'estimates'. As the following suggests, writing down high estimates of unknown, unregistered home educating families is futile:

> **Q46 Chair [Graham Stuart MP]:** Do you have any ideas on numbers, because the previous Committee concluded that there were 20,000 registered and that there were probably a minimum of upwards of 45,000 who were home educated. I was on that Committee, but I cannot remember on what basis we came to that number.
> **Jane Lowe:** There was a lot of nonsense at the time.
> **Neil Carmichael [MP]:** Why am I not surprised?
> **Jane Lowe:** This is really funny, because we were told about the number of unknowns. Well, how do you know anything about an unknown?
> **Damian Hinds [MP]:** Politicians do.
> **Q47 Chair:** I think estimates were made by various people, weren't they?
> **Jane Lowe:** Guesses.
> (House of Commons Education Committee, 2012, p Ev 7)

Even 20,000 as a lowest and known figure is much more than those being educated in alternative educational philosophy schools which are small schools of often less than 100 places. Whilst most alternative schools are fee paying, home education is without fees. It may involve an elective financial hit for a family due to probable loss of a parental income and other additional expenses that end up falling onto parents' shoulders. A common example of these expenses is examination entrance fees, although there is new potential that examination fees may be paid by the state for EHE children (see House of Commons Education Committee, 2012). EHE, unlike a private school, does not involve paying a business to take over where state-provided schooling has failed or did not deliver. It is quite literally and significantly *do-it-yourself.*

The main focus of this book is about discovery by adults of EHE, although sometimes mention of discovery of other alternatives will be made. Such mention involves schools like Sands and Summerhill. The options taken have in common that they maintain a legal relationship to compulsory *education* (not schooling) for children. Discussion of what exactly compulsory *education* entails is made later in its specifics.

Kuhnian discovery as a framework of discovering EHE

Kuhnian discovery applied to education is when people realise in a profound and impactful way some new piece of information, after anomalous experiences, confusion and searching. A period of confusion leads to the formation in their minds of an altogether new concept. In the case of the parents in the research study on which this book is based, the discovery in question was that they did not have to send their children to a school. School-based problems were often the cause of their search. Or, they simply discovered, with joy, that alternative ways of being educated other than mainstream schooling existed for their children. EHE, in particular, was an option found and recognised as viable, with good indications for successful outcomes (Kunzman and Gaither, 2013).

In terms of parallels with a Kuhnian theory and framework for discovery in the natural sciences, the moments described in the context of questions and interviews about education were startling in their similarity. The same kind of discovery moments happen in both arenas. They happen in the same ways, as a 'switch' from an old paradigm of information and concepts, to a new world of information and new ideas. Discovery in the natural sciences and the social sciences occurs in the same manner. Some implications for the science of education are drawn out and discussed in the chapters to follow.

What is perhaps most important about the existence of such a 'switch' as it relates to education are the transformative effects that experiencing this switch creates. But there are other ideas to take from these situations. Briefly (and this is discussed in greater depth in Chapter Four), the switch means a form of revolution. It involves 'shifts in perception' (Kuhn, 1962, p 113). Kuhn also used the phrase 'world changes' to conjure up the impactful nature of these occurrences. So, for adults confused about educational options and possibilities, discovering that education without schools is legal *and* viable can change their world. Not only is the change conceptual because the concept of what education can be and actually is changes, but it is also literal in a practical sense because it changes the way one lives one's life and sees the world and self (Sheffer, 1995; Neuman and Avriam, 2003).

This transformational experience of concept leads to *personal* transformation. This is discussed further in Chapter Four in relation to Foucault's theory of technologies of care for the self. Transformation occurs because the personal is built on and by virtue of conceptual tools which allow self-expression, meaning making and understanding (Elliott, 2007). Thus, if concepts change so too does the personal experience of the content of those concepts with ramifications in personal life. In the interviewees' descriptions of the discovery of alternative educational possibilities, the onlooker is '... confronting the same constellation of objects as before and knowing that [she/] he does so, [she/]he nevertheless finds them transformed through and through in many of their details' (Kuhn, 1962, p 122). Transformative effects manifest in lifestyle, social attitude and ontological perception of self in the context of the world. A small moment of realisation is all it takes: 'an experience of a fleeting but momentous event' (Ward, 2008, p xi). This moment of realisation has implications for educational studies, discussed in chapters to follow.

So the study takes ordinary people's experiences of a particular kind to do with education, focuses in on a key moment that changed their views about it and their subsequent choices and practices, and then brings this to bear on what education is seen to be and what it *can* be seen to be.

I aim to open up education through the telling of the story of these moments. That sounds simple but it is also, actually, astonishing. The reason for the astonishment occurs on a number of different levels. First, discovery happens mostly by chance and through luck in individual lives. It might never have happened at all, yet it is life changing in a largely positive way. Second, it offers a new way to understand educational studies. Third, it both threatens the format of current societal democratic functioning but also might offer help to what is a currently incoherent 'project' that is not yet democratic *enough*. There is much more also involved which will be touched upon. It is as though these moments are a fulcrum of some kind in our current and potential educational world view. That sounds grand, but it is surprising what relevance they have for education as a whole.

A scandal?

Outcomes from the 'moment data' of the study are to be analysed for their fascinating nature as touching so much and with surprising interdependent coherence. Yet, attention must also be paid to the difficult data that emerged from these moments. Parents were clearly indicating that they want to know about alternatives to mainstream schooling.

What I mean by mainstream schooling is perhaps obvious to many, but a brief clarification is required: the schools that 98–99% of children attend in England, whether fee-less or fee-paying. The usual model for such schools is variation on a model of regular slots of enforced teacher-led learning and the system it requires to function in this way. The school uses authoritarian methods to maintain control and has strict hierarchies of power with the headteacher in charge, followed by layers of management moving through (and down) to a beginner teacher; beneath whom sit students, who possibly gain more power and prestige as they get older. Other school staff are indeterminately placed in the schooling hierarchy but they too use forms of authority and hierarchy to make sense of their workplace. Children must attend lessons and they have little choice over what they learn (after potential subject choices). They are required to comply with standards of learning and behaviour and complete tasks such as homework, in regular and conformist ways, on pain of sanctions.

Parents want to know what it means to educate without such a school. Furthermore they cannot understand or condone that state provision and educational information is so limited. This applies whether they are actively and happily choosing to look for alternatives to mainstream provision or if circumstances are pushing them into alternative solutions.

The parents and adults I spoke with expected, demanded and wanted information. They clearly cared about their children's education and its outcomes of all kinds: academic, social, psychological, spiritual and so on. Education mattered to them. They did not necessarily want to understand alternatives fully or even in part, but they did not like ignorance about their options. Often, and scandalously, not having this information was causing people sleepless nights, fear, anguish, anxiety and stress. Some people cried when they told me of their relief at, for instance, chancing upon a newspaper article outlining the option of home education.

As a researcher I often felt that I had stumbled into an uncharted territory of the harm that schools do to individuals. This was the story of parents who are not heard and do not know where to turn. Child voice exists as an idea but parental voice for parents legally responsible for a safe and happy, successful education for their children was being ignored for the sake of maintaining a system that could not take their concerns into account. Despite organisations such as *Parent Partnership* – an organisation of advocacy on behalf of parents whose children have special educational needs and statements – the depth of the harm schools were doing to some parents was not being recognised by schools. Discovering the way out from school attendance was, as one interviewee, Pippa,[3] put it: 'the light at the end of the tunnel'. It was a moment of relief and release from genuine suffering for too many of the people I spoke to who had taken emergency recourse to home education practice. Such situations belied the use of the word 'elective' in the now commonly used terminology. This is a common problem of EHE as a last resort – especially it seems with children who have special educational needs (Parsons and Lewis, 2010).

Although not all home education is strictly speaking 'elective' this book refers to home education with English terminology as discussed in the Badman Report (see Chapter Three), where the term elective home education (EHE) is used. EHE is also known by other names such as 'home schooling', a term more prevalent in the US. Within EHE there are many styles. In this book, I will be referring mostly to a style of EHE which does not follow the pattern of 'school at home', and which is known as autonomous EHE (see Thomas and Pattison, 2007). This style is also known by other names such as 'deschooling' or 'unschooling'. Such a form of EHE is characterised by freedoms for the children to self-determine their own learning, as discussed in Chapter Three.

Apart from parental suffering caused by schools, the study also highlighted that discovering education without schools is legal can be a scandal in other ways. The story and the issue is one of a class-ridden society where largely only the already privileged and well-educated are deemed to deserve and be suitable for education without schools. These people often don't think that 'other' (read poor and uneducated) types of people ought to know about EHE. Such judgements come also from relatively affluent people in official capacities in local authorities. Affluent, well-educated parents use their knowledge to exit the school system properly, following the right protocols.

On the other hand, children seeking initial escape from schooling in the form of truancy and school refusals are not treated as having an alternative option, when a legal option to not attend schools is in line of sight. Their parents are punished by a lack of information and prejudice against their fitness as potential home educators. Instead of outlining legal options as a solution to dissatisfaction with schools it is assumed that the only way forward is to take – or threaten to take – parents (who do not have knowledge of EHE as an option) to court for their children's non-school attendance. Those parents with greater cultural capital such that they know about EHE as an option, or those lucky enough to have discovered the law, are protected from this. These people can cite their rights as parents in England to take recourse to an alternative education without schools. But many are being coerced into unnecessary negative situations because they are being treated as *not* having the option to develop EHE practice; something 'given to' and used easily by the affluent, culturally wealthy or the informed. *All parents* have these options but this is not explained widely. When it is explained it is often because headteachers want to get rid of a disaffected and troublesome child (House of Commons Education Committee, 2012). So EHE discovery is a political territory linked to social equality and political justice.

Conclusion

These issues are very complicated and they are discussed in depth later. In Chapter Eight I offer a way out of this political, social and educational quagmire of discovery by offering a framework of classification involving three discovery categories. The categories take account of two minor categories and one major one: (1) negative discovery (abuses of the law) and (2) excuse discovery (in other words, no real initial wish to home educate but it avoids the problem of fines and threats of a prison sentence) and (3) the majority occurrence of genuine discovery – parents who have found the other world of EHE and take action to become informed. The demarcation made between discovery rationales offers policy makers, local authority officials and others ways to navigate this difficult area.

So education without schools is not a small matter of minor concern. Finding out about it, as the data in Chapter Five testifies, is life changing. A small-scale study focused on cognitive '*augenblick*' realisations in the minds of ordinary people highlights this. This book looks at why, how and what information about education without schools might be made available. The impact of a change in our concept of education as not *just* schooling but *also* alternatives without schools is considered. What happens when we give parents more knowledge about how education can happen for their children? The possibilities are significant and could alter our educational scene as well as our politics, our society and our futures.

Notes

[1] Home education law differs slightly in Scotland and Northern Ireland in respect of permissions for deregistration but in all four nations it is fully legal and possible.

[2] The Badman Review of 2009, which was a government commissioned report on EHE in England and which made controversial recommendations for changes to registration and inspection of home educators (see Chapter Three), discussed numbers. A more up-to-date resource is Fiona Nicholson's www.edyourself.org website.

[3] All names of interviewees used in this book are pseudonyms.

TWO

Against educationism

Opening up to education as modal

Education is a plurality of possibilities. Yet, amazingly, at a deep conceptual and structural level this idea seems currently not yet to be in place. Some say education has even been foreclosed; that we exist enframed by a dominant and dominating discourse, deeply anti-democratic in its nature and perhaps irredeemably so (Flint and Peim, 2012; Peim, 2013). How do we know if education does lack structural, conceptual diversity? Because major end users of educational services – parents – do not yet have the idea or the concept of education as *modal*. Modal refers to education as a model or models. There can be many modes; each made of valid differing methods, theories and practices. That there are many also signifies that they are iterative: open to development but also flexible to various openings, closures, changes, challenges, morphing and blending. They represent – in a Derridean sense of permanent possibility – what is to come, rather than what is programmed and already given (Lees and Peim, 2013). Educationists are, I believe, professionals of educational research and practice *charged* with informing parents (as an end product of their activities as thinkers, researchers, practitioners) about such flexibility in the educational landscape and the options it would open up.

Yet, educationists themselves – teachers and researchers at every level from the school to the university – struggle to comprehend how diverse education can be. Many even struggle to be interested. Educationists conflate education with schooling on a regular basis: they forget about modal diversity; they do not demarcate strong differences (Lees, 2012). Has a mainstream schooling mentality strangled the science of education? Is it totalising and shutting down the educational imagination? What hope for parents then to be aware of options? Yet, education *is* modal. It can function in different worlds which each have their own coherent accounts of theory and practice, working harmoniously and homologously. There is a point of transition between these modes: a switch moment. This will be seen in the data presented later. On account of the movement from one world of education to another that we see in that data, we know that there is more than one mode.

A one-mode picture – education as non-modal – offers an experience in which education suffers from a kind of 'educationism'. This is a prejudice against forms of education that are outside of the standard model: different *races* or *bodies* of education are treated differently, with some regarded as more valid than others. Levels of validity afforded are aligned with proximity to the acceptable one-model norm. One EHE parent, speaking to the government committee gathering evidence for a report about EHE provision (which will be cited often in this book), notes:

> The new jobs created to support EHE families ... consist largely of ex-teachers (with a fundamental belief that school is the best place for children) or social services worker who aim to steer families back onto the school pathway ... LAs are not at all interested in recruiting qualified and/or experienced home educators to these advisor posts. This is no different to excluding a disabled person from a role which involves offering experiential support to people with disabilities. (House of Commons Education Committee, 2012, p 11)

Educationism is prejudice and actively so. It acts to exclude validity for different approaches to education, putting one model in the place of diversity. Examples of educationism against EHE are rife. The evidence from HEAS to the House of Commons Education Committee states that 'Deep-seated prejudice against home education is widespread' (HEAS to House of Commons Education Committee, 2012, p Ev 40). Paula Rothermel clarifies in an aptly titled article 'Home education: practising without prejudice?' that prejudice against EHE most often occurs because officials do not follow extant procedures and law appropriately (Rothermel, 2010). Educationism assumes that EHE is inadequate, inappropriate or even just plain wrong. EHE is seen as needing the 'ways' of mainstream schooling to inform it; to set it on a straight path and to 'allow' it to operate. The pressure to conform to a schooling mode is often intense. Where this operates as a force it is vandalism.

Educationism can also involve aspects of implicit and explicit bias, such as the concern regarding harms against children in EHE which often taints mainstream public discussion about it as an option (see for example Conroy, 2010; Lees, 2011a). The following comment, by another witness giving evidence to the Education Committee, is an example of this bias playing itself out. This is seen to occur in EHE in much the same way that other groups in society may fall under suspicion of crime or negative deviance, solely on account of particular superficial features which draw prejudicial attention (such as teenage boys walking in groups, wearing hoodies):

> How are we ever going to break down this culture, which has been touched upon by a couple of the members of the Committee, where people should not have to feel that they are automatically under suspicion of doing something dreadful to their children? (House of Commons Education Committee, 2012, p Ev 6)

Different 'bodies' *of education* from mainstream provision   dressed as that provision is in teacher-led learning, hierarchies and authoritarian structures, timetables, ability streaming, assessment and set work – suffer from distorted, prejudicial perspectives and ignorance projected onto them. Other educational practices are of another model and mould. They look different; act different. They are different. It is education, just as *all* humans are people independent of their appearance and physical self; other kinds of education from the mainstream hegemonic model are still education. But just as people are discriminated against and perceived through a lens of prejudice based on their basic human body and even attributes (such as accent or clothing), so too education of a kind other than the mainstream is deemed less educational, less valid, more problematic. The views on it are as difficult and an aberrant function in similar ways to human body based prejudices, but in another arena. It is educational prejudice at a structural (epistemological, ontological and political) level of what constitutes the educational.

Acting differently

Other modes of education act differently from the colonising idea. The children play and work according to their moods and interests. Learning happens through spontaneous conversations and discovery. Children choose for themselves how and what they want to understand and for how long they want to study. This is true for autonomous home education (Thomas and Pattison, 2007) just as it can be true for thorough-going democratic schooling (Neill, 1968; Goodsman, 1992).

Non-whites, the disabled, the working classes and others different from the normal and normalising – the regulated (Foucault, 1977; Hacking, 1996; Foucault, 2004) – have suffered historical (and contemporary) injustices requiring legal recourse and constitutional change around the world. So too those participating in home education and thorough-going forms of democratic schooling have had to apply to the courts, to appeals, complaints and review procedures to uphold their educational rights – the right to be *educationally* different (Summerhill School, 2000; Stronach, 2005; Children, Schools and Families Committee, 2009; Stronach, 2010). The consequences of this can be profound: hurt, heartache, failure of valid projects, fear, backtracking and lack of support from officials, inadequate development of ideas on their own terms and subsequent damage to the full flourishing of a home educated child. It can cause educational trauma, leading to lack of success in outcomes, de-motivation, damage or stress to relationships within the family, negative and draining personal effects on self-esteem, failure to thrive on usually valid educationally-otherwise terms, and so on and on. Educationism is serious. It deeply affects lives.

If it is true that different educational worlds are at play, functioning, delivering, operating and acting in the lives of people, then the modern world is full of educational options. Yet education as provision in society seems ossified. It is simply too deeply *stuck* in one mode. Improvement agendas of the one main model act to sediment and perpetuate this situation (Harber, 2008; Flint and Peim, 2012), as do 'what works' agendas if these act according to underpinning, determining assumptions about education (Biesta, 2007). The consequences of such ossification are not just a light-hearted question but can go to the heart of what a democratic peaceful and flourishing nation can be (Harber and Mncube, 2013). I suggest in this book that education is stuck and dogmatised into one hegemonic conceptual model; one mode of the mainstream school. I suggest furthermore that this is educationally tragic and deeply damaging to human society: a limited vision with limiting outcomes.

Although it is the case that to the sides of this dominant model are many diverse options, this situation of options to the side is not education itself. We need another model and structure to apply to our common understanding of education. If diversity at a deep level is to fructify and develop true educational *options*, we need education as modal. The hegemonic force of the main model is currently the power that determines who is in and who is out in terms of educational modalities. All means of education seem touched and tainted by the force of the mainstream. Yet, the data here mirroring Kuhn's scientific paradigm shifts hints that this huge goliath of *a paradigm that comes from the mainstream school* may merely be the first paradigm of education we have so far encountered and widely recognised. It can and probably will be overturned, with time. This is the case if education functions paradigmatically at a structural, not merely a methodological level. I explain later more fully what is meant by that, highlighting why such change is so important: change through understanding education differently but also the active change that education as modal brings. Alternatives and their discovery lie at the heart of such change being possible.

Why opening up the idea of educational choice at the level of the mode is important

The following quote from Michel Foucault suggests some of the territory that the discussion to follow will touch upon:

> In short, I think we can say that in and of itself an act of knowledge could never give access to the truth unless it was prepared, accompanied, doubled, and completed by a certain transformation of the subject; not of the individual, but of the subject himself in being as subject' (Foucault, 2001, p 16)

Choosing education for oneself and especially one's children is, or ought to be, 'an act of knowledge' accompanied by personal development. The reasons for this lie spread across the vast territory of the effects of education and its status as a very new science (Condliffe Lagemann, 2002; Labaree, 2006). The educational modality that was experienced in the past by any parent when of school age is in a state of flux because education is not a fixed given. The experience of education which formed children who then, in time, have become parents can be reassessed when those parents encounter education as adults choosing for their own children, because educational practices and philosophies can change. Changes can open for parents new vistas of being and becoming if they perceive that educational practices have moved on since their days at school, or that even knowledge regarding education has developed since the time of their childhood.

Because the nature of education is to be (naturally and inherently) troubled by many temporally determined social, political factors and new awareness emerging from continuing research, it is in a constant state of new beginnings and new possibilities; or ought to be. But current openings witnessed in educational studies and schooling practices – such as democratic functioning – seem so terribly slow to make it into schools in an active way (Harber, 2009a; Harber, 2009b; Harber and Mncube, 2013). Education, whilst troublingly fluid, seems continually fixed and stuck – and we can easily behave with it according to such a limited vision – but is that because of a failure to see it as it really is? As modally diverse? Clearly education *can* change and educational difference is available. Embracing that difference is 'a transformation of the subject' (Foucault, 2001, p 16) because the eyes of awareness have opened, as shown in Chapter Five. The child of such a parent can thus benefit from state of the art educational practices and theory rather than a tired and *assumed* model, functioning beset with problems. A revolution in the self can occur, as new awareness of what is possible educationally emerges into consciousness. Education as schooling can then *not* be taken for granted as the only way forward.

Parents can transform themselves through educating themselves about education; through finding out information. What else is education good for? Yet, vox pop data from a small-scale street based survey (see Appendix for methodology) gathered during the study mentioned above, highlighted that parents and other adults rarely consider multiple forms of education. They make no 'acts of knowledge' when it comes to education. Parents are not demanding a broad spectrum of information of the government. They are not *awake* to or sufficiently *aware* of the deep inadequacies of the one-model system offered nor of the inherent fluidity that education offers for self-formation. Education is at the heart of the relationship of the self to other, so as an enlivened, broadened concept it has potential in and also beyond the personal. Greater knowledge regarding educational options at the modality level has potential for better, more awakened citizenry given the general care that the majority of adults have for their children. Certainly the data on the transformative impact of discovery of alternatives in Chapter Five shows such awakenings occurring. The interviews tell us these adults have been awoken from a slumber of political, social and educational assumption.

For most people education means one thing: school attendance. That *not* going to school might be possible for a child is often a challenging and shocking idea, demanding a readjustment of their view of the 'social contract'. This is especially true for citizens of countries like Germany where home education is illegal, as it is elsewhere also; although in native English speaking countries around the world it is widely legal. German adults – all of whom have attended school – rarely entertain the concept of not attending school, because school attendance in their home country is compulsory. Failing to attend school is punishable without exceptions. The idea of education *without* schooling is ridiculous for them. Perhaps this reaction to education without schools is to be expected if no exposure or legal structure allows for the idea to develop. But in England *not* attending school is possible and has been inscribed in UK law since 1944 by the Butler Education Act. Section 7 of the 1996 Education Act is the up-to-date version and is relevant for England and Wales:

> The parent of every child of compulsory school age shall cause him [*sic*] to receive efficient full-time education suitable –
>
> (a) to his age, ability and aptitude, and
> (b) to any special educational needs he may have,
>
> either by regular attendance at school *or otherwise*. (Emphasis added)

Yet, many adults in England cannot conceive of education allowed without schools. This is a sign of an education that is not functioning through modal awareness. It shows an ignorance of legal possibilities that apply to England and indeed the rest of the UK. I consider that were the following street survey to be conducted in any other country in the world where EHE is legal and valid as an educational option (except perhaps the US), similar data would be found. It would be the same because the conflation of *the idea* of 'education' with schooling as an assumption is global and runs deep. Parents have little knowledge of education as modally diverse. They have only ever been told about education as formed by one modality and no doubt most have only ever experienced education as underpinned by that mentality of the school. The following data testing the idea of conflation of education *as* schooling in the public consciousness is from 2009 in England.

The street survey

The initial question in each street survey interaction, asked to all the respondents was: 'Did you know that (your child) children don't have to go to school?'

> **Respondent 56:** It's the first time I've thought about it ...

> **Respondent 2:** Oh my God! I really didn't know. I really did feel it was illegal. So why are people going to prison? ... I'm amazed.

Respondent 81: Yes, I did know. Home tutoring. I've read it in the newspaper at some point ... Yes it was a surprise. I thought kids had to go to school. I have no real feelings about it [*re finding out*]. I think it's up to the individual.

Respondent 43: I thought it was just in America. I've never heard of it in the UK.

Respondent 80 [*Parents together*]: Mum: No. I thought it was compulsory. I didn't realise that. Dad: I didn't know that. Damn, if I'd known that I wouldn't have gone to school. [*Dad looks at me fearfully to gauge my reaction.*] HL: Does it come as a surprise? Mum: Yer.

Respondent 29: No! That's ridiculous. How are they going to learn?

Many of the street survey respondents either voiced that they wanted more information for themselves or felt that others should be told it was an option. A common thread running through the interactions was that people thought the government should provide more information about EHE as an option and that would be more fair and right.

Respondent 12: More people should know about it because the pressure is on people all the time ... It's very misleading isn't it. You do think it's law because that's the way it's put across to people ... I'm quite surprised that it's not the law [*that people should be told about EHE*]. Everything is drummed into you that you need to send them to school by law. We even get letters that lead you to believe ...

Respondent 14: I think there [*are*] more people out there who don't know. I think it should be more widely spread or known. I like the fact it's an option. I think the government should tell people. I've never been told. [*Found out via article on Melinda Messenger – a celebrity who home educates.*]

Respondent 38: I don't think people know. They think they have to send their children to school. It's not widely discussed. There doesn't seem to be a great deal of information about it. It's not discussed due to work [*that the state wants people in work*].

Respondent 17: I'm glad [*to be*] aware there's a choice. It solidifies that viewpoint: I'm sure this is what I want [*mainstream school attendance for her child*].

Respondent 88: Yes. They can be home-taught. It means they don't have to go to school as long as their parents can provide an adequate education for them. I don't agree with it. I think children need socialising ... I think it's something people should know so they've got the choice about whether a child goes to school or they teach the child themselves ... Yes, I think the government should advertise it. Maybe they should put a few posters around ... have a spot on the local news. [*HL: Any reason why they might not do that?*] They might ... because of [*Khyra Ishaq*] they're frightened because it's not secure ...

There was also a degree of anger shown by some who, faced with school-based difficulties, realised their knowledge of educational options fitting to circumstances was limited.

[*This respondent was having difficulties getting the school to agree that she could take her son out of school for short trips to see his father, who lived in another part of the country.*]
Respondent 33: No National Curriculum? It's quite good [*to know about it*] ... Now I know I can educate him at home there's not a problem. It's a good idea. Now they can learn their way ... I mean ... who needs algebra!

Respondent 7: [*He looks deeply thoughtful and angry.*] The average person doesn't know. It seems there's a lot of benefits that you don't know unless you're ... [*looking tearful*] I just wish I'd known that a while ago. It makes me feel guilty now. [*Sister was badly bullied and the family were at a loss to know what to do.*]

Many of the street survey respondents knew something about EHE as an educational option but these individuals appeared to the researcher (HL) to be affluent from a quick, glancing (subjective) judgement. Those respondents appearing (superficially) as less affluent did not have this knowledge at their disposal, except rarely. Often people who thought they knew about EHE as an option had a distorted picture: for example, they thought it was teachers coming to the house or did not understand that there are ways for children to learn that do not involve regular teacher interaction. (See Chapter Three for discussion of the nature of autonomous EHE.)

If this small sample is in any way representative of the general population, parents in the UK are significantly ignorant of the lawful range of educational modality, practice and philosophical options open to them as parents with legal responsibility for the education of their children. Here are some further examples:

> **Respondent 41:** I didn't know. I thought they had to go to school ... surprised ... I thought they get punished if they don't go to school ... truancy ... I thought they had to be taught in some way even if it's home tutoring.

> **Respondent 54:** ... through ignorance. It's not a well known fact. I was in the right moment at the right time watching the TV. It's more promoted to send your child to school, isn't it.

> **Respondent 73:** No. Obviously school should be compulsory for all children: need good education for career, social aspect, be in stable environment. [*HL: Does education mean school?*] I suppose so. Obviously there is home learning ... [*HL explains it is a legal option for all parents.*] I maybe thought automatically that home education was for special circumstances to begin with. I wasn't totally aware that everyone could do that.

> **Respondent 88:** [*Found out about it*] when I was training to be a nursery nurse in 1996. Before that I heard about it on the news.

> **Respondent 69:** Vaguely. I knew there were other options but I didn't know they didn't have to ... I got the impression it was something they'd have to fight for.

What the street survey was aiming to research was levels of awareness of the possibility of EHE as a valid, legal option for parents; as an idea that was realisable as an option. It aimed specifically to test *the nature* of that awareness. In other words, what were the boundary lines of people's understanding? Of course, a great deal of other interesting data came out of and subsequent to this key question, but the 'trap' of the first question acted like a gauge for levels of discovery. The following interaction aptly shows how this was highlighted by the nature of the first question: 'Did you know that children don't have to go to school?':

> **Respondent 58:** No. That's the normal thing to do. I thought everyone had to go to school ... I knew home education existed. The way you say the question. I said no: it's the way you say it. If you had said 'Did you know home education existed?' I would have understood where you're coming from.

What this interaction shows us is that there is a gap between knowing home education exists and *realising* that home education is a possibly normal and acceptable mode of education and an option. Because children don't have to go to school it is *theoretically* normal. The reality however is different. It is marginal practice with little conceptual airing in wider society. The normal practical concept of education is schooling. It is the realisation of the normalcy of the possibility (see Stevens, 2003b, for a discussion of EHE becoming 'normal') which constitutes part of 'genuine' discovery of EHE (or other alternatives to the mainstream) discussed later. Simply *knowing* is superficial knowledge without relevance to practice. This could tip into the 'negative' or 'excuse' discovery categories in the right/wrong circumstances. (See Chapter Eight for discussion of discovery kinds.)

Is discovery a good idea?

Two indications from the discovery of alternatives that the street survey created[1] with its first question are: (1) knowing that profoundly different educational options are available is welcomed by adults; (2) when they feel there is genuine choice of ways and philosophies of education to take place, they feel that the choice they make – which is mostly for mainstream schooling – is validated by their freedoms to decide. Discovery might be said to set them apart as citizens *democratically choosing*. They become different from those people who suggest that feeling obliged to send their children to a mainstream school was a limitation on their ability to engage not only with themselves but also their society (Neuman and Avriam, 2003).

Of course, how viable an option EHE is as practice was something else that came out of the street survey. Levels of ignorance about what EHE is or actually can be were high. As were, frankly, prejudices. It was often seen as hippy, weird and only for the abnormal/subnormal.

This is very far from the truth. This is educationism and an assumption that comes from modal ignorance. There might be an argument to say that one cannot viably do something unless one understands it to an operational degree: whatever that can mean. A removal of ignorance and prejudice is required for a concept to be clear enough to use on its own terms and not those of prejudice. The most repeated prejudice about EHE as educational practice in the street survey was to do with a perceived lack of socialisation opportunities, which is a myth I touch upon briefly in Chapter Three.

But the issues ranged over a wider territory. There was a strong sense coming from the respondents that school was beyond reproach *as* education itself. It was not often questioned as the right place for education to happen or as the right conduit for education as a social enterprise. The interactions were all short so it was not possible to go into lots of detail about the reasons for these often very strongly held views about schooling as the 'one' answer. To the researcher's mind it was clear that there is a substantial mythology about schooling in most parents' mind that is rarely, if ever, reconsidered and mostly only when problems occur.

Yet, educational choice that is real choice – choice not circumscribed by social, political expectations and demands, as well as possibly a quiet and deliberate lack of information provision – is perhaps a realising of ourselves; a technology of the self, which I discuss further in Chapter Four. Just as education can offer the possibility of engaging with people for self-realisation of many kinds, so the mode or model of education must fit the individual, not a norm. To think like this is socially challenging. These days we manage our affairs through labels of the 'normal' (Hacking, 1996). Some see difference from succumbing to normalising forces as being emergent and true; unique and irreplaceable (Biesta, 2006). But perhaps this vision is somewhat naive with regard to this difficult arena of educational *modality* choice. We are all shaped and forced into certain moulds. The issue is the degree and nature of that moulding; its constraining capacity and the ends to which these forces aim or do constrain and how. Also, what we do about being moulded.

An education that offers a way forward through freedom from substantial constraints and which can allow the self to emerge organically is often found outside or without a school. The reasons for this are manifold. Key ones include schooling as involved in unceasing improvement agendas (Flint and Peim, 2012), expectations of socialisation (Medlin, 2000), and standardised and conservative pedagogic formats (Children, Schools and Families Committee, 2010). These are all encapsulating powers and forces upon the self: demanding, shaping and determining. Escaping these powers on and in the personal is for some parents an imperative. They want their children to be free to ask 'Who shall I be?' and for the answer to be an open one. They want them to be free of heavy school pressures and to grow naturally, not within a mould or according to a 'shape' that may or may not be a good one. But this is not easy to achieve in current society with its limited view of what education is and can be. But it should be easy. The law supports that.

Such freedom from being moulded by education raises controversial issues about living in a democracy (Apple, 2000a). These require us to ask what responsibility we might have to share common values and to work together according to similar principles of educative upbringing (Reich, 2005). Yet, there are also other issues connected to these questions that are about democracy: what freedoms do we actually have and in what way can we realise them? EHE is seen by many practitioners as the right to facilitate democratic freedoms of being oneself, naturally, and not being forced into a state-created, 'preferable' ideal (Glanzer, 2008). EHE is often seen as a last refuge from state interference in various ways that impinge on the growth of the self: be it ideologically informed by philosophical or religious beliefs (Knowles et al, 1992) or pedagogically inclined to do with styles and ways of learning (Thomas and Pattison, 2007).

Of course EHE is *ironically*, despite its supposedly democratic context, also possibly the greatest anarchist style 'people power' scenario relating to education there is. It is perhaps politically and socially structurally close to the philosophical underpinning of anarchist education (see Suissa, 2010) without outwardly declaring anarchist politics. Many home educators speak warmly of anarchist ideas, even if they might choose to vote Conservative. This ought not to belie the diversity of educational practices however because some EHE practice is extremely traditional in nature; every family is different. Biesta points out, in his analysis of Jacques Rancière's egalitarian politics, the nature of scenarios which avoid top-down 'vertical relationships' as having – according to Rancière – anarchist tendencies (2010, p 41). EHE is a classic example of the dissolution of the kind of top-down relationships that are found regularly in mainstream schooling (Sheffer, 1995; Thomas, 1998; Dowty, 2000), as are the other thorough-going democratically inclined alternatives mentioned previously (see for example Fielding, 2005; Fielding, 2013).

This presentation here does not consider that the discovery of EHE is some kind of anarchism in action. That view is informed by the research participants' lack of formal identification of the act of discovery with anything political; for them it was and is a personal, emotional and perhaps, in some cases, a spiritual event (albeit without being in the context of any known creed). We see some of these tendencies and characteristics clearly in Chapter Five. Discovery of EHE may come as a result of different triggers, such as parents taking the initiative and looking for a new way to do things, the desperation of parents over an untenable school situation, a philosophy of education or other motivations, such as a chance encounter. It is not a new political movement. What is discussed later however is its status as a potential new human rights issue.

Conclusion

Diverse educational modalities are in operation. They show education is paradigmatic in function. Not just at the level of methodologies and research philosophies but at an epistemological level of the structures of education as they are formed through interweaving theories, philosophies, histories, cultures and practices. Education is paradigmatic because it is formed of many possible modalities. There is a switch moment or point of transfer between them – this means whole worlds to discover. Just as with Kuhn, incommensurabilities are in play between paradigms (Kuhn, 2000a), which is discussed further in Chapter Four. Factors of incommensurability cause and perpetuate educationism.

Realising the modal or paradigmatic nature of education is a new understanding that is potentially transformative for people. We do not yet have circulating in society a *diverse* concept of what education is and can be that is mainstream. The moment of discovery which takes people from one world of education into another, is the key to turn the lock; to bring true diversity into education. But it is a secret key.

Because much education is for the educating of children, parents are key players in the realm of whether education is modal or not; important agents of discovery and change. Parents as guardians of and legally responsible (within English law at least) for their children's education, want to know what education as modal means and what it indicates for them and their children in practical terms. Of course, they might not talk about it in that way. Instead, they might ask to be informed about educational diversity at the level of means, methods, theories and practices. They want to know about education beyond a vision of a school. They ask (and I believe educationists have an obligation to explain): 'How can education not be a school? How can it not be in a school or part of a school?'; 'What change to education inside or outside of schools is actually possible in a deep-seated way?'

These questions underline that what educationists and their policy counterparts currently offer and do *is not diverse enough* at a modality level for the major social market consumers of educational services and science. Education has come to be known as the school and the school as education in the same way that Judith Butler identifies that:

> ... certain kinds of practices which are designed to handle certain kinds of problems produce, over time, a settled domain of ontology as their consequence, and this ontological domain, in turn, constrains our understanding of what is possible. (Butler, 2005, p 309)

We need to say more about education. We need to discover more. There is more that is possible than we currently understand and new understandings will take time.

Note

[1] Further data from this survey is available here: http://etheses.bham.ac.uk/1570/1/Lees11PhD.pdf (pp 202–8).

THREE

Why is elective home education important?

Introduction

This book focuses in on discovery of EHE in particular for three reasons: (1) its radical difference, as a location for education, from school attendance of any kind; (2) the fascinating and important confluence of social, political, ethical and educational issues which meet at the juncture of EHE; (3) the common ground that EHE shares with other 'alternatives' in terms of theory and practice and the marginalisation of these practices within a mono–paradigmatic educational world view.

When referring to educational alternatives it is useful to note that this phrase can often be used as a term for settings outside of schools, but run along the same mentality lines as mainstream schooling. An example might be a pupil referral unit. By alternatives I do not mean this kind of provision, and I do not pay much attention to what alternative settings of the 'mainstream' there may be. The use of the words 'alternative' or 'alternatives' points here to radically other ways of understanding and practising education as distinct from mainstream pedagogical *assumptions* involving hierarchy and authoritarianisms. 'Alternative' is often associated with progressive education theory and practice – described by Röhrs as an holistic pedagogic and democratic approach of the whole person supported by national localised practice and an international and historical movement for educational development, albeit largely aiming to happen in the mainstream with regard to access of resources at the very least (Röhrs, 1995).

In previous chapters I introduced the idea that education is currently seen as one modality: an essentially *non*-paradigmatic vision at a structural level, which is developed further in Chapter Four. Educational studies and its practices allow considerable diversity but control the well-spring of differences from one core place by virtue of a limited vision. That place is education but it is still, to a large degree, determined by a 'traditional' chalk-talk, desk-based idea. But this is a false vision of what education is and can be. I will now expand on the three points highlighted above, which underpin why EHE is a significant part of an *other* vision of education. Features of the contemporary contexts for discovery of EHE in England are highlighted.

The lead up to the 'signs of concept' that the empirical research data (to follow in Chapter Five) allows, is a slow journey of preliminary discussions. For this data to be able to speak *on its own terms* (and not those of the school), substantial prior underpinnings to secure a solid basis for new understandings advanced are first presented. That this takes time is inevitable because the matter is complex.

What is EHE?

EHE is different. In terms of common ground around the world, EHE is simply about being educationally active, largely without a school. When I speak of EHE in England, much has resonance for other countries, but some features, events and implications are naturally unique to English law, just as some communities of home educators are recognised features of other countries. An example would be conservative Christian home educators in the US (Kunzman, 2009). The extent of difference and common ground in EHE, wherever, is unique also to each home.

As touched upon in the previous chapters, I refer in this book to radical difference from a mainstream schooling mentality: in particular a form of EHE known as 'autonomous home education'. Many home educators report that a 'school at home' mode moves towards and into aspects of a more heutagogic (self-directed: see above and this chapter) and autonomous form of learning with time (Safran, 2008). The sheer variety of EHE practice from home to home means that any definition is short of the mark. For instance home educated children may flexi-school (Gutherson and Mountford-Lees, 2011), which means that they may go into a school as a registered student for part of a school week only. The status of flexi-schooling in England is, at the time of writing, undergoing debate. Or, they might temporarily register (for example to do assessed course work) with a school or college for the sake of exams. They may sit at a desk at home, for set hours, each day, and be taught algebra and stanzas or tectonic plates and UK citizenship, or they might roam the woods building hideaways one week and explore a project on peanuts, astrophysics, social stigma, or any other topic, the next. It is impossible to stereotype home education content because it is so unlimited in scope and potential nature. It might also follow the National Curriculum if deemed useful.

The personal, familial nature of the home lends itself to dissolving strict boundaries around learning, including traditional ideas about what a curriculum constitutes (see Doll, 1993; Davies, 2009). Moreover, fluidity of this kind is both healthy practice and rather inevitable to some degree with EHE, especially as it evolves as education on a daily basis (Thomas, 1998). Once a fluidity of attitude is thus achieved, structured 'book exercise' learning can nevertheless return and even be requested and enjoyed (Thomas and Pattison, 2007).

Because the educational practice is located in the home as a base and not in an institution, personal dynamics around home education are very different. Children awake in their educational site, they eat there, they conduct their intimate private lives there and they experience their education outwards from this base, rather than as a result of split-site attendance. It is not true that home educated children spend all their time at home. In fact quite the opposite is often the case. Children and parents utilise the broad spectrum of social facilities and local sites and amenities to discover educational opportunities (Thomas, 1998; Hern, 2003; Hern, 2008). So, whereas schooling is predominantly site-based except for occasional visits out, home educated children roam around learning, developing and receiving understanding in new places all the time. All of this means that the educational dynamics are different.

The dynamic of what and how bodies move in relation to learning is other. The fact of not being locked into a school system's rules means that features of the educational experience are different at psychic personal levels of self-expression. EHE children don't wear a uniform (unless they want to); they wear their own clothes. EHE children don't have to carefully police what they say, who they say it to or particularly how they speak; they don't have to strategically plan where they sit and who they sit next to – they are largely 'at home' in body and mind. This ease is a part of alternative education philosophies and experience (Stronach and Piper, 2008). It is not part of schooling (Foucault, 1977; Henry, 2013).

How the children based at or exploring out from the home learn is also very other than a school learning mentality. Coming to understand something can happen gradually and then explode into quite advanced awareness quite quickly. There are no necessary and linear 'key stages' to follow bit by bit. No required tasks. No homework to report back on set learning duly undertaken. Of course, this can change if autonomous home educatees want to work in that way, but it is not enforced or coercive. A core area where this difference is obvious to home educators is in the spontaneous nature of reading readiness and ability. For example, surprising scenarios are possible. A child could one day pick up a Roald Dahl book and laugh, yet when asked what she finds funny she might comment not on the pictures but on twists in the storyline, using words spoken out loud from the text – this without her parents previously being aware she could read at all. Such examples are common; part of the educational scene (Thomas and Pattison, 2007; Thomas and Pattison, 2013). Concentration on a particular topic, such as bridge engineering or a musical instrument, can mean that some EHE children develop advanced skills in certain areas and perhaps at a much earlier age than most school children. The lack of timetabling in EHE means this is facilitated in ways that a school system obstructs. Such a method to develop one's learning helpfully questions – but can also miss benefiting from – the given base and common skills of learning that a (nationally) set curriculum can offer.

Social experiences are different from school socialisation. Whilst some EHE children suggest they might want more friends (and perhaps even might consider school attendance for this end), EHE children do have friends. It might be that their friendship group is smaller than that theoretically available in a school: through local EHE groups, boy scouts or girl guide groups, swimming clubs and so on, they meet and make friends. The benefits of EHE with regard to social experience lie mainly perhaps in the expansive nature of the age spectrum of people with whom an EHE child might become friends. They are not locked into a set age group due to year groupings and the narrow-mindedness this can inculcate. Exposure to a diversity of people brings their human experience into close, everyday proximity as a learnt and teaching aspect of the world (Knox, 2008).

The dynamics of any learning from 'subject' teachers is also other. Parents serve their children sometimes as didactic teachers but this can be a relationship the children themselves find unworkable. If it isn't working for the children, parents soon acquiesce to another way because educational (and personal) life becomes challenging. Even if they aren't at first sure what that is, ought or could be, they can come to realise that a hands-off approach might be better (Dowty, 2000). After an often initial phase of parents seeking to replicate the look and feel of a school at a substitute school desk, with text books and set tasks, the learning teaching protocols of schooling (inevitably perhaps) dissolve into a more fluid and organic scenario (McKee, 2002). Conversations of educational importance take over: 'spontaneous conversation, both incidentally and sometimes at great depth' (Thomas and Pattison, 2007, p 7). The walls of the school have at such a point come down. New educational concepts and behaviours are in play.

Common ground between EHE and schooling?

What remains that is common across all education and what is predominantly found in this educational land without schools, is important to understand. When the historically sedimented structures of the school system collapse in the face of the strong intimacy of the home education setting (Merry and Howell, 2009), what is left that is *essentially* educational? EHE is altogether a very different human experience of education for a young person than regular school attendance. Yet, is there something that these two settings and dynamics share? The answer lies in many places. The core of the matter is potentially in the self-development that both venues promise and deliver. However, home educated children are frequently heard to suggest that it is easier for them to be themselves and develop in a way true to themselves without schools (Llewellyn, 1993; Sheffer, 1995; Llewellyn, 1998). Going against so much rhetoric about the promise of schools is the sad fact that sometimes schools disappoint in this regard:

> People believe that through education[1] they can remake their lives; talent can be found anywhere, hope kindled in the harshest places. Expectations of what education can and should offer are constantly rising. The second message, however, is that education can also deliver disappointment and frustration. It's not good enough to get more children into school, if few of them learn and what they learn makes little difference to their lives. (Leadbetter, 2012, pp 23–4)

Happy and successful self-realisation is what one would hope to find as an educational essential, whatever the location. But structures seem to matter fundamentally for what is essentially *educational*. There is plenty about schools which is not educational but something else: a tacit curriculum of social, not educational formation (Bowles and Gintis, 1976; Willis, 1981; Reay, 2001). In such a light, schools are not education, they are schools. EHE is not education, it is home-based practice. But EHE is *more* educational in this core area of focus of realisation of the self as opposed to the realisation of 'results', that schools see as important (see for example Sheffer, 1995).

A 'what works' educational policy approach is said to matter, although this emphasis is contested for its democratic deficits (Biesta, 2007). We can look to EHE to see that *dismissing* 'what works' is of value. EHE highlights more of the intrinsic purpose of education and focuses in on what Biesta calls the purpose of the educational, where community, democracy and deep meaningful engagement with self and other are part of the educational worldview (Biesta, 2006). EHE practices of educational freedom are in contrast to rife instrumentalism of a schooling mentality (Delandshere, 2001). The common ground is found to be 'what works' but rather than for policy makers and their portfolio, what works for a *particular* individual. Schooling is organised, it seems, by distant bureaucrats with bright ideas imposed on others without much consultation. EHE is often deliberately unorganised and close at hand, for known and respected adults who listen to the particular child to respond to interests, questions and facilitate learning.

The place to be to know what education is

This book focuses on EHE because it is, research wise, *the new and cutting edge* place to be as a modern educationist. If educational research struggles with knowledge of issues around equality, diversity, teaching and learning, social impacts, political policy tensions, the law and education, psychological readiness, teacher relationships, home/school relationships, facilities and resources, texts and technology, power and its perversions, democracy in hierarchies and so on, and on, EHE has something to offer that illuminates all of these and more. The relevance of EHE to all educational research might come as a surprise to those who see it as minority practice and whose interests lie in schooling and other areas of education. In EHE however, there are fundamental questions to be explored, with ramifications for whatever we can mean by educational, in the past, present and future.

For a start, EHE lays bare the meaning of *getting* an education. If a child doesn't deliberately learn to read during childhood yet, at age twelve, suddenly cites a broadsheet newspaper article *she has read* on economic development challenges in the context of economic downturn, was she receiving an appropriate education when aged seven or eleven? She couldn't read then. Did that mean she wasn't getting a 'suitable and efficient' education? This phrasing of an appropriate education being 'suitable' and 'efficient' (and full-time) comes from Section 7 of the 1996 Education Act and was focused on in the Badman Review as not being 'defined in law' (Badman, 2009). The current English legal ruling and latest official government advice to support this is that the child needs to be fit to take part in her community as what we might call a contributing, useful adult, or be enabled by her education to choose involvement in other types of community in the future if she wishes (House of Commons Education Committee, 2012).

That she cannot read aged eleven is irrelevant to this framework. She was developing those skills as she went along without needing a reading programme to assess and measure this. Attempting to measure and programme her reading education is to misinterpret what happens and eventually occurs. *Not* measuring challenges schooling attitudes to testing that are now unfortunately all too educationally prevalent (Peim and Flint, 2009). These attitudes are based on fear, whereas EHE works, successfully, with trust (Safran, 2012). So outcomes from EHE which are, by schooling standards, weird, offer new perspectives on educational value and practice.

There is much to learn from the *how* of how children in EHE learn that is relevant for new curriculum developments. Freedoms supposedly inherent in the nationwide Scottish Curriculum for Excellence initiative are found in EHE (see Lees, 2013a). The value of spontaneous conversation is a profound area for all educationists. It undermines our idea of teacher-led learning if children can learn just as much as in a school – to the point that they develop as rounded and effective individuals and social citizens – 'just' from everyday chatter with adults and others, as they can do with EHE (Thomas and Pattison, 2007). This outcome, reported by home educators and educatees, challenges the *need* for the school, if a caring family environment and parental attention is available. Of course for those children who lack this background, schooling can remain a vital source of support. Beyond the family, in countries without institutional educational resources for all such as India, there is a recognition by educational pioneers of outreach projects that: 'If you don't have a school you can still have learning' (Chavan, 2012). Research projects there have proved this in surprising ways. For instance, placing an internet portal in a wall in a rural area may result in coming back to find children fluent in advanced new skills (Mitra et al, 2005). These matters are discussed further in Chapter Seven.

The implications of this are extremely exciting for education in terms of overturning well-trodden assumptions and myths about the desperate need *for a school* of some kind for all children to gain an education. I call this dominant idea 'tyrannical' (Lees, 2012). The tyranny of schooling as the sign of education is a large part of globally targeted programmes of 'education' for every child, from UNICEF and other organisations such as the Qatar Foundation. This is despite their understanding of the need for education also without schools. As we see above, being desperate for schooling and bemoaning its absence need not be thus. Autonomous home education as successful education is an exciting possible educational pathway forward for most children if their parents agree. Its internationally applicable principles open it beyond the homes of the affluent to the developed world and we need to understand this potential better through rigorous research. The scope for cost-saving with good educational outcomes is, of course, huge but not well understood.

Other aspects of this form of education are to do with relationships and power. The way matters are decided in autonomous EHE is not about power dynamics. Parents say they seek to facilitate their children's natural curiosity; offering them freedoms to explore, to investigate, to find out and to resolve. They aim to interfere as little as possible with this. For such relationships to work in harmony within a household, discussions are had that function without top-down orders from parents to children who must obey. Negotiation is important. This is much closer to the democratic meeting of Summerhill and other such democratically organised schools (Fielding, 2013) than mainstream schooling. School systems could gain value from what I call here positively and with admiration the disordered but solid achievements of autonomous EHE, if they could just embrace the 'restless encounter' of the democratic (Fielding, 2009) implicit in its unconstructed nature; allowing themselves to be thereby deconstructed.

In social and political terms, EHE is the place to find passionate educational conversations. It's not a boring zone. As Conroy states: 'Discussions around home education excite quite visceral responses on all sides ...' (Conroy, 2010). The reasons are manifold but they link to the law, human rights and the idea of the family, parenting, children's rights and much more. Specifically Article 26(3) of the United Nations' Universal Declaration of Human Rights: 'Parents have a prior right to choose the kind of education that shall be given to their children' and Article 2 of Protocol 1 of the European Convention on Human Rights:

> No person shall be denied the right to education. In the exercise of any functions which it assumes in relation to education and to teaching, the State shall respect the right of parents to ensure such education and teaching is in conformity with their own religious and philosophical convictions.

The UK sought a qualification of the second sentence of the Article – now in force in Article Two of the First Protocol of the UK Human Rights Act 1998 – at the time of signing in 1952 (see Merrills, 1995, p 117): so long as it is compatible with the '... provision of efficient instruction and training, and with the avoidance of unreasonable public expenditure'.

So, home educating is compatible with extant human rights protocols (see Farrell, 2012). Yet the reality for those who discover EHE has been and continues to be difficult in many respects. Whilst perhaps hard to personally live, this creates an enlivened field of research. Contentions in the UK are primarily safeguarding concerns, official registration, what constitutes a 'suitable and efficient' education (curriculum and teaching issues), socialisation and educational marginality. A big issue with regard to human rights for American home educators is religious freedoms, which some commentators debate around matters of democratic inclusion, individual participation and common citizenship contributions as well as realistic possibilities for exit to other ways of life (Apple, 2000a; Reich, 2005; Glanzer, 2008; Kunzman, 2012).

For home educators in the UK comfortable with the idea that their human rights are protected by and in the UK, discovering they have to fight for a human right – which is what they consider is the nature of their wish to home educate – can be 'surprising' (personal communication with long term home educator, November 2012). All of this deep-seated controversy and indeed, intrigue, adds to why EHE is important as an educational issue. It brings to the fore so much about education we can take for granted with a schooling model. Some examples of this contentiousness are now explored.

EHE in contention?

As mentioned in Chapter One, EHE is a legal choice for parents in England. In 1944, the Butler Education Act established that children could be educated 'either by regular attendance at school or otherwise' and this enshrined in statute the possibility for home educators in England to pursue their chosen method of education. Since this time – despite legality – EHE has been through a series of local acrimonious court cases due to a lack of understanding of EHE on the part of local authorities.

The *Harrison* case in the late 1970s/early 1980s is a famous UK example.[2] The parents of five school-aged children, all with severe dyslexia, chose to home educate them in an autonomous style. Threats from the local authority ensued, including the threat of taking the children out of the family. The debacle subsequently ended in a court battle to ascertain whether these children were receiving 'efficient full-time education suitable to their age' (Harrison, 2010). The situation ended with a partial yet unsatisfactory resolution that at least offered the family some protections.

Connected to this story of a local authority threatening a family with judicial measures on account of their desire to home educate, EHE started to emerge from the shadows. Education Otherwise (see www.education-otherwise.org) was founded by Iris Harrison and Dick Kitto in the light of the Harrisons' experiences (Harrison, personal communication, circa 2010) as an advocacy and information service for parents wishing to home educate. This charity has continued to grow over the years since, at the same time as other organisations relating to EHE have emerged throughout the UK. There is now a proliferation of web-based EHE groups, most of which advocate in some way on behalf of EHE rights and reason.

The legal choice to home educate has seen challenges technically outside the law or, in being made, challenges to its diaphanous boundaries and significations in ways that have tended to be disrespectful and dismissive of EHE as an educational option *even though it is protected by statute as an option*. Such challenges often took lengthy and painful wrangling with the authorities to establish the *practiced* and practical right to home educate. Court cases such as the *Harrison* case have now become unusual in England: parents are no longer threatened with their children being removed from their care, *solely* because the parents wish to home educate. Such court action and rulings continue elsewhere, such as in Germany. However, unfortunately, it is not yet the case in the UK that safeguarding issues – emerging mainly from social services concerns for the physical, emotional and mental well-being of children – and EHE as educational practice are rationally divorced. Conroy discusses this (2010) with reference to the Badman Review (Badman, 2009) discussed below.

The same difficulty was again raised in 2012 with local authority home education official Melissa Young, by the Education Committee looking at support for home educators. Placing EHE in the right area of council functions, to avoid conflation with safeguarding concern, is an issue:

[*Explaining where her remit as EHE officer sits within the council.*]
Melissa Young: I am not the only minority group that sits within that umbrella. If you are looking at the Virtual School as having a role, we have children in care; we have, on that roll, children subject to a child protection plan and children in need; but we also have those that maybe at certain points in their educational life may require some support from either Careers or –

Q152 Craig Whittaker [MP]: I understand that, but surely you would be better placed in a mainstream schools scenario.

Melissa Young: The Virtual School sits within the 11- to-19 achievement division.

Q153 Craig Whittaker: It does, but if I was a home educator and you were coming out to see me and I knew that you sat within that looked after children/safeguarding area of the council –

Melissa Young: We do not see it as just safeguarding. We are promoting the educational achievement of all children within the Virtual School, and a lot of what we do is data-tracking for those children in care, but we are also looking at the educational attainment and achievement of those home educated children. Obviously, we take safeguarding very seriously, but it is not all about that.

Q154 Craig Whittaker: No, I get that, but what I am trying to refer to is the perception, though, that home educators would have with you sitting in that area. It was just a comment.

Melissa Young: I have never had an issue with it to date, and I think I have a positive relationship with the home educators we have within Warrington, as I said. I think once they have met with me and they understand the support that I can offer and that I am a listening ear, then it is not an issue.

Q155 Chair: Do you see the point though?

Melissa Young: I can understand, yes.

Q156 Chair: We have a suggestion that perhaps it could be placed in the library service rather than in the education department. The education department is all about schools, so people with a school head come and assess you to see whether you are running a home school when you are not; you are home educating. The aim is that home education should not appear when you see lists of risk and various things as it does sometimes in safeguarding. It suddenly appears on the list as 'home educated children', as if there are safeguarding risks when there is no evidence of that. Well, I do not know. Do you think there is evidence that home education is a safeguarding risk factor?

(House of Commons Education Committee, 2012, p Ev 24)

Significance of the 2009 Badman Review

The Badman Review was commissioned by the government to look at EHE in England. It is a perfect storm of context for discovery of this form of education. It – no doubt unintentionally – raised the profile of EHE as a possibility, via media reports on the Review. This began with a press release announcement including an unfortunate implied – if unintentional and simply careless, EHE-*ignorant* – call to distrust EHE parents' care of their children; carried through on the grounds that they might be abusing their children or forcing them into early marriage (Frean, 2009). No doubt the intention was to raise awareness of what I call in Chapter Eight 'negative discovery' by some (abusive) parents. Genuine home educators (see Chapter Eight for a framework of what is 'genuine' – briefly here I mean all who are involved with *active* home education practice) understandably reacted with horror.

The media coverage of this announcement is anecdotally said to have stimulated discovery of home education in the public. Calls to the *Education Otherwise* (see above) helpline rose during the period (personal communication). The high media profile of this controversial review highlighted and discussed, in the public domain, the fact that children do not have to go to school. Some people were pleased to have heard of a choice separate from schooling. The debate from all sides underpinned the idea that EHE might be feasible and valid as an educational option. Yet, the intention of the Review was not to stimulate a higher profile for EHE but to establish 'a balance between the rights of the parents and the rights of the child' (Badman, 2009, p 3).

Numbers are crucial to understanding EHE significance. This was possibly a key reason for the Badman Review in the first place, in order to change local authority registration practice to capture accurate numbers:

> It is a matter of some concern that despite a number of research studies and reports, it was not possible to identify with any degree of accuracy the number of children and young people currently educated at home. Our own data concurred with the DfES (2007) report, that there are around 20,000 children and young people currently registered with local authorities. We know that to be an underestimate and agree it is likely to be double that figure, if not more, possibly up to 80,000 children. (Badman, 2009, p 22)

The law currently allows for freedom to not become a statistic in the practice of EHE: registration is not required *de facto*. It happens either voluntarily or as a result of system protocols such as a school informing the local authority that a child has been deregistered from the school by their parent/s. As mentioned in Chapter One, we do not know how many home educators there are in England. It has been suggested that Badman's potential 80,000 estimate is far from the mark, and ought to be lower.

Although discovery by parents was theoretically made easier by the Badman Review publicity just mentioned, the exponential year-on-year rise in England during circa 2005–09, of home education take up at approximately 17%, has perhaps now levelled off. It now seems to sit at an increase of around 1% a year of local authority EHE registrations. This however does not capture families whose children are born, never registered with a nursery or school and then go on to be home educated. The figure of 1% is based on freedom of information requests made by Fiona Nicholson of *Edyourself* (Nicholson, 2011). Schools Minister Elizabeth Truss told the Education Committee in October 2012 that figures were not held centrally and that there were no plans for the DfE to change this (House of Commons Education Committee, 2012). Despite the Badman recommendation, compulsory registration for all home educating families did not make its way into statute.

The Badman Review set out to consider the question of regulation and monitoring of EHE in the light of fears that children were being kept without appropriate socialisation opportunities, were not being sufficiently and effectively educated in a full-time manner, or were being abused in some way, under the pretext of being home educated. Specific concerns included that the law, as it then stood, disabled local authorities from making what they said were appropriate checks. This was underpinned, the local authority (LA) said, in relevant guidelines (DCSF, 2007) which made clear that entrance into the family home and the right for authorities to demand to see the child or children being home educated was not permissible. A particularly controversial suggestion in the Review was the idea that children could be interviewed in the family home without the presence of a parent or guardian 'if deemed appropriate' (Badman, 2009, p 40).

The Review itself was criticised and challenged on a number of grounds for a lack of appropriateness. Specifically, robustness in statistical claims was called into question and also the schooling mentality it used to assess EHE, philosophically and as practice. A Select Committee enquiry looked at these issues and reported disappointing problems with the Review's conduct and conclusions (Children, Schools and

Families Committee, 2009). Academic contributors to the Review also criticised it for its lack of robustness, quality of methodology and presentation and its 'populist' pandering (for example Conroy, 2009; Conroy, 2010; Stafford, 2012).

With significance for educational group action and activism, the English home education community went up into political 'sixth gear' in 2009. They aimed to thwart, in particular, the recommendations to register on a yearly basis (EHE practice being dependent on the local authority's permission), the local authority to have legal right of entry to the family home and the interviewing of children without a parent present. They saw these recommendations as especially intrusive, but were generally distraught about the manner, timing, conclusions and recommendations of the Review as a whole. There was a significant minority in the home education community who made themselves very loudly heard in protest through various tactics. Yet they were not alone. A normal response to a Select Committee enquiry consultation, post-review, is said to be in the region of 100 submissions and this consultation took over 5,000. This gives an indication of the generalised wide extent of the response and the level of concern. The action showed how important EHE as a preserved free right was and is for many people.

For the purpose of this book's focus on discovery, two aspects of the Review stand out. There was no *explicit* detailed consideration of the significance of rising numbers of those home educating. It was a silent subject in the Review. Yet rumours and academic mention of significantly rising numbers were rife at the time. Rising numbers of home educators are, of course, connected to discovery of EHE. Nor was there discussion of provision of suitable materials by local authorities informing parents of EHE as a possible option. Information is at the heart of discovery. The latter omission indicates further that knowing about educational modality options is not even on the radar. It does not seem to be *wanted* on the common radar. This underpins points raised earlier about education functioning as though it is one paradigm of the school with school-like or un-school-like affiliates, but with no fundamental paradigmatic difference to mention. Thus, information about non-existent (not recognised) difference is seen as not needed, despite the attention of a sweeping, impactful government review on educational 'difference' and its debacle. The matter of information silence is discussed further in Chapter Six.

It seemed from the emphasis on home education as a possible 'abusive' scenario and scene of potential educational neglect, that the review process wanted to – or was at least not afraid to – blacken the name of home education. This is significant as a case for an understanding of how education is used and abused – manipulated through spin in the hands of politicians and their policy vehicles, whether well intentioned or not. Certainly, as soon as the review was announced, *all* newspaper articles about EHE in England changed in tone. There were, subsequent to the Badman Review debacle, no positive media articles on EHE as a 'wonderful' way for education to happen. Yet this had been a noticeable feature and tone of newspaper articles and other media reports in England on EHE prior to Badman, when EHE had been almost universally painted as an interesting, beneficial and viable educational modality and option (Phillips, 2004; Rogers, 2005; Argument, 2007; Blair, 2007).

The Badman Review abruptly closed down media interest and communication regarding educational choices in the public arena. This made discovery less likely to flow from chance media encounters. Such encounters with media articles and reports by parents were shown in the data of the study this book refers to, as a significant route for enthusiastic EHE discovery and take up. A sudden new negative public media profile for EHE might lend some light to an eventual drop in rising take-up numbers. It also raises – if not answers – the question whether a reported high level of exit from schools into EHE (see Chapter Seven) in the pre-Badman years was fixed or stemmed by the Badman Report. We are unlikely to ever know if it was a deliberate plan to thus negatively portray EHE. Whether it was intentional or not, it would seem that affecting the media's perception of EHE is a successful way to knee-cap discovery given that any active (positive) state information provision is missing.

Still being confused?

The conflation of EHE with safeguarding remains a difficult problem. Despite extended debates such as that discussed above and substantial numbers, in the millions (Princiotta and Bielick, 2006; Kunzman and Gaither, 2013) of home educators around the world existing, conflation persists as a global confusion and geographically comparative problem (see Eddis, 2007). A tragic case with connections to parental choice about home education is that of a child called Domenic who was taken into care in 2010 in Sweden, on what seem to be spurious safeguarding grounds.[3] Political asylum was temporarily granted in the US in the same year to a German EHE family on the basis that they were being persecuted and threatened with the removal of their children into care (Frean, 2010; Moore, 2010).

Perhaps because of the 'bad' history of the Badman Review debacle with the home educating community in England and beyond (although community is a necessarily loose term when applied to EHE practitioners), there is now more awareness of the danger of conflating safeguarding with home education practice. Following on directly from the same Education Committee session quoted above, witnesses called to discuss facilities and support for EHE were very reluctant to get drawn into safeguarding discussions. The following dance around the matter shows this:

> **Q156 Chair:** ... Do you think there is evidence that home education is a safeguarding risk factor?
>
> **Melissa Young:** That is a leading question.
>
> **Elaine Grant:** The remit for today was not to discuss safeguarding.
>
> **Melissa Young:** My title is Virtual School Education Manager, and I think it is clear to parents what they will be getting when they engage with me.
>
> **Q157 Chair:** So, Elaine, you are not comfortable answering that question.
>
> **Elaine Grant:** No.
>
> **Q158 Chair:** That was not an invitation not to do it.
>
> **Elaine Grant:** It was not what I came today prepared to discuss. It is a very, very inflammatory element of home education.
>
> **Q159 Chair:** It is, but is there evidence that home education should be a safeguarding risk factor?
>
> **Helen Sadler:** No more so than being in school.
>
> **Chair:** Precisely. Anyway, I do not give evidence. I always encourage my colleagues not to start giving evidence when they are asking questions, so I shall try to resist. Thank you.
>
> (House of Commons Education Committee, 2012, p Ev 24)

Statutory EHE guidelines to English and Welsh local authorities were introduced in 2007 (DCSF, 2007). Then came guidelines to Scottish local authorities (Scottish Government, 2007). This showed signs that EHE had become, after a fashion, an accepted feature of the educational landscape. So, it would be expected that improvements in England in relation to conflation of EHE with safeguarding were in place. Yet the above quoted debate clearly shows this is not the case. As this book discusses, EHE as a concept of educational difference is not an easy one to filter through to mainstream awareness. Due to this difficulty it certainly does not – cannot – happen overnight. The process is obviously and inevitably painfully slow. Also, I suspect, receiving little help.

Only isolated champions seeking justly to take EHE out of safeguarding concerns, take action. The Chair's closing comment above is such an action. Safeguarding is not an EHE issue. Safeguarding is a safeguarding issue (Rothermel, 2010).

EHE has too few friends with any 'institutional' power. However, the following – again from the same evidence session – is an intriguing exchange about 'championship' between the Chair of the Education Committee Mr Graham Stuart MP and Elizabeth Truss MP, who is at the time of the exchange, newly appointed to Parliamentary Under-Secretary of State, Department for Education:

> **Elizabeth Truss:** Well, I think the right objective is trying to get the best possible service, but that is an objective that does not lie in my hands in the Department for Education. That lies in the hands of local authorities, and it is for leaders of local authorities to tell this Committee how they see themselves measuring up to the best local authorities in the country in terms of providing these services. It is for them to say, 'Well, how could we be better at delivering the services? How could we co-operate rather than having a more difficult relationship with home educators, and how could we learn?'
>
> The fact that the Committee is undertaking this report is good, because it raises the profile of the issue; it will make local authorities think about what they do. I am sure that they will be extremely interested in the recommendations that the Committee provides. But I think we have to be careful in all this that we do not think that the Government doing things is a panacea that is going to solve problems on the ground or going to deal with issues on the ground. In this structure we have at the moment, whilst it may look imperfect and it may not look as logical and structured as one might think it ought to be, it is, broadly speaking, working. We have to be careful not to upset that balance in terms of the responsibility that home educators hold themselves, the responsibility local authorities have with respect to SEN [Special Educational Needs] and the responsibility that the Government has as well to make sure that home education is taken into account when we are

putting through major pieces of legislation and so forth. So I do not believe there is some kind of utopian solution here.

Q256 Chair: Will you be a champion of home education within the Government?

Elizabeth Truss: Well, obviously, it would make me very popular with the Chairman of the Education Select Committee.

Chair: Never a bad thing.

Elizabeth Truss: Never a bad thing. I certainly very much respect the decisions of home educators to educate their children. I think we have a good system that is sustainable, and I will take up their cause with other Ministers in my Department, as well as with myself.

Q257 Chair: You will take up issues with yourself. I look forward to those broadcasts.

Elizabeth Truss: Those discussions are for internal purposes only, I am afraid, and they are not FOI-able.

Q258 Chair: So will you be a champion of home educators within the Government?

Elizabeth Truss: Yes.

(House of Commons Education Committee, 2012, p Ev 36)

The Badman Review was the start of a new focus in England on EHE as an important minority issue, but it had a strong negative focus on safeguarding that did not adequately take into account the voice of EHE. That EHE practitioners (and their concerns) are too easily ignored is highlighted in another quote from the Education Committee session:

Q233 Chair: I think we are less concerned about intrusion on parents, if that were to be threatened. We are talking here about local authorities, whose practice, whose paperwork varies widely, and we have a minority group spread all over the country. One of the reasons I am interested in them is because they are a group with no electoral bite anywhere, too small to be significant to anybody apart from themselves, a marginal group, very easily ignored, and treated by departments that, in certain authorities, do not take this area seriously and are rather careless both of the law and their duty to provide. There is a risk of that, so it is an interesting case study as to where there might be a

need for some challenge, and localism alone, certainly at the ballot box, is unlikely to lead to improvement.
(House of Commons Education Committee, 2012, p Ev 33)

Sidelined by difference

One of the contributory reasons to being 'very easily ignored' might be the marginal position of alternative educational modalities within education as an academic arena. A question posed to Professor John Furlong of Oxford University at the Birmingham University School of Education Student Conference in 2009 concerned EHE and the Badman Review, which was active and in the news at the time. His reply was that he could not answer the question because he didn't know any background to the issue and furthermore was not supposed to, nor did he need to know about the issue raised: 'I don't need to know about alternatives because they are alternative', he said.

Whilst from his perspective this may seem reasonable as an individual, it is also telling. It exposes a generally widespread (albeit not exclusively) attitude of ignorance and dismissal amongst prominent educational academics to alternative educational modalities. It is a contention of this book that this is a failing of education as an academic discipline. As a discipline it ought to know education better: as a whole, not just what is known as mainstream.

Knowing about alternatives is increasingly being shown as educationally relevant, through business and social entrepreneurship innovations around the world. For an educationist to *not* understand how people are making up and self-developing their own 'mainstream,' is to ignore the learning, studying interests and activity of millions of the poorest people in the world, especially in some of the most populous countries (see Waks, 2012). It is to rest with the mainstream of the western privileged and see only through their educational eyes. *Other* eyes see alternatively. There are, of course, many forward-thinking educationists who see with other eyes, even if their underpinning politics might not align (see for example Mitra et al, 2005; Andreotti and Souza, 2008; Tooley, 2009; Macfarlane, 2012). This is discussed in Chapter Seven.

Comments and thought that sideline these alternatives from mainstream consideration suggest what I started with in this chapter: EHE is important for education beyond its current self. There is then a need to maximise the issue of EHE as education, for educationists. It can open a gateway to better appreciating innovation – a more open-minded mentality suited to the future and its needs unknown.

Showing common ground between EHE and other radical alternatives?

Previously I mentioned the commonality between schooling and EHE. This was the promise of self-realisation, with potential uncommon outcomes. To take this idea of commonality of theory and practice, promise and premise, into the realm of alternatives alone – to compare between alternatives – is also of interest. Yet, to discuss all the possible common ground that EHE has with other alternatives in terms of theory and practice is no small ambition. They have lots in common: love of freedom, privileging the whole person, enjoying emotional literacy, interest in democratic communication, and so on. It is valuable to understand why EHE, and other forms of education without the mainstream school, work as an 'alternative team' in being a choice away from schools (of a mainstream modality). For reasons of space, I can only hint at how this occurs and point to its significance and implications for educational studies.

What can be said is that where education functions progressively or alternatively, it has been noticed that 'an astonishing degree of unanimity is discernible both in questions of fundamental approach and in the results obtained' across various such international educational projects (Röhrs, 1995, p 23). Models (modes) with autonomy as a premise tend to work in the long term without need for fixing or change (Stronach, 2010). EHE is like this in its ability to self-regulate its way to an equilibrium of success over time. This 'journey' seems available to any who take the autonomous EHE path (Sheffer, 1995; Thomas, 1998; Dowty, 2000; Thomas and Pattison, 2007; D'Marea Bassett, 2008).

Educational alternatives have common ground in perhaps two places. First, the form of education is heutagogic, not pedagogic or even andragogic. Heutagogy is a term coined by Hase and Kenyon (2000) to describe self-directed learning that is 'an extension' of Knowlian andragogy (adult man/woman andr-agogy, as differing from child ped-agogy). Knowles suggested self-directed andragogic learning was:

> The process in which individuals take the initiative, with or without the help of others, in diagnosing their learning needs, formulating learning goals, identifying human and material resources for learning, choosing and implementing learning strategies, and evaluating learning outcomes. (Knowles, 1975, p 18)

Hase and Kenyon identify 'a linear approach to learning' in this which they believe can be surpassed by taking 'account of intuition and concepts such as "double loop learning" that are not linear and not necessarily planned'. (2000). Their vision of learning is more 'restless' (Fielding, 2009) and 'disruptive' (Leadbetter and Wong, 2010):

> It may well be that a person does not identify a learning need at all but identifies the potential to learn from a novel experience as a matter of course and recognises that opportunity to reflect on what has happened and see how it challenges, disconfirms or supports existing values and assumptions. Heutagogy includes aspects of capability, action learning processes such as reflection, environmental scanning as understood in Systems Theory, and valuing experience and interaction with others. It goes beyond problem solving by enabling proactivity. (Hase and Kenyon, 2000)

This is something which many alternative 'pedagogies' – or is 'heutagogies' more appropriate? – value. Although alternatives are not obliged to be heutagogic in nature, the freedoms of non-institutional bases can offer democratic proclivity for the unsettled exploration of what is *intuitively* right in a given place, time and with particular people and circumstances.

Second, the way all alternatives are marginalised *on their own terms* within a mono-paradigmatic educational world view is common ground. As I have outlined, there is currently an education for all – as individuals but also as a global agenda – but one centred on the mainstream school model of authority and hierarchies.

Other terms of educational engagement and conduct, belonging to alternatives, are about freedoms and disrupt pedagogy as teacher-to-student. Given the description of EHE above in this chapter, what stands out from the practice is its spontaneous nature and its flexible form. Little is necessarily preordained and if it is, this is part of a set of goals that are continually up for negotiation. A similar form of educational attitude and practice is found in democratic schooling around the world (Bennis and Graves, 2007).

This model of freedoms without licence (Neill, 1966) is based on thinking which believes in giving children choice about their learning and voice in their community but also demands community responsibility for self and others. Choosing what and when to learn but also being aware of the consequences of one's choices, is a common feature of the curricular approaches of both democratic schools and autonomous EHE. A meeting to allow concerns and comments amongst the community to be voiced is common in democratic schooling (Fielding, 2013) and listening to children's wishes as well as airing concerns within a family is common to EHE (Holt, 2003; Thomas and Pattison, 2007; Safran, 2012).

I suggest not being accepted *on its own terms* of the educational is a common experience for all alternatives because – as Thomas and Pattison suggest in their research of informal, autonomous home education practices – there is an insufficient vocabulary of and for other educational theory and practice at present. It does not have a language of its own to make linguistic and thus conceptual sense on its own terms. Terms and forms from the mainstream are co-opted to attempt to communicate difference:

> The constructs used to describe and explain formal education are not only irrelevant but themselves create barriers to moving our understanding forward. A large part of the difficulty in discussing informal learning is our lack of accurate and meaningful vocabulary. Whilst preferring to eschew such terms as "teaching", "the learner", "curriculum", "engagement," we have, nevertheless, found ourselves often forced into using them for lack of alternatives. The moment is perhaps ripe to develop a new vocabulary based on a new epistemology of learning. (Thomas and Pattison, 2013)

Such trouble is shown and manifests in events of challenge against alternative educational forms. Incommensurability between language and understanding takes place (Lees, 2011a). Two recent infamous examples of alternative education overcoming, overturning and disrupting incommensurable difference of this kind are the Summerhill court case against Ofsted which was won by Summerhill (Summerhill School, 2000) and the Badman Review discussed above.

A final further intriguing similarity in this brief survey of commonalities within alternative education is the general high levels of happiness and joy heutagogic/pedagogic freedoms and the concomitant lifestyle they seem to bring. Students from democratic schools and EHE mostly – and this is notable about alternatives – say they like what they educationally do and the effect it has on them: 'I like how I've learned, I like who I am, and I like what I know ... I'm going to like to be like whoever I end up being' (Sheffer, 1995, p 97). That an educational 'world' can significantly deliver such a result is important. It ought not to be ignored by educational studies.

Conclusion

Combined, the elements above form another world of education or other worlds. EHE is a world of difference, educationally speaking. What is clear from the numbers involved in (autonomous) EHE and similar alternative practice is its minority status. This stops such an education gaining a foothold in the mental imaginary of the everyday adult and parent, where mainstream practice is so well known.

Yet, such practice exhibits a theory of education: 'A theory of education is a comprehensive, coherent, and internally consistent system of ideas about a set of phenomena' (Knowles et al, 2005, p 10). The package shows promise to be effective for learning, growing, developing, being, becoming, acting, engaging and sharing in and for the lives of growing children. It is flexible and therefore fit for a technological age of rapid expansion and social change (Hase and Kenyon, 2007).

This book discusses why many find it hard to offer respect and understanding, intrigue and interest to alternative education. There is a difference about EHE in particular that people can find sufficiently disturbing that they may prefer to ignore it or, they may have just never heard of it. There may also be elements in mainstream dismissals of EHE practice which are connected to patterning of social behaviour, whereby common patterns are those followed. Unusual anomalies literally do not fit into what is acted upon and enacted (Bentley et al, 2011). What all the other people do is the right thing and appropriate. Being unusual, sticking out, seeming strange, is to be avoided and dismissed as an option. Whereas, falling into or choosing another path is for those who are in psychological pain, feel uncomfortable and need alternatives (Hase and Kenyon, 2007).

So the difficult courage of EHE as education of difference in a 'normal' and normalising world is important. But because many people *do* use it around the world, there must be something happening there worth sticking one's neck out for, worth discovering.

Notes

[1] Note the common conflation of education with school attendance that is involved in this excerpt which when in context is clear – 'education' as a term here is referring to schooling. The present book of course disputes this very common, unhelpful conflation.

[2] *Harrison and Harrison v Stevenson*, Worcester Crown Court (1981).

[3] *Johansson v Sweden*, European Court of Human Rights: Application under Article 34 of the European Convention on Human Rights and Rules 45 and 47 of the Rules of Court, June 2010. An update to the *Johansson* case at the time of final editing in 2013 is that, unfortunately, little has been resolved.

FOUR

The theory of the gateless gate of home education

[Responding to a brief explanation of the theory of the gateless gate of EHE discovery, at HESFES – the yearly Home Educators' Summer Festival:]
Illona: Yes, I see that and coming here, I see it even more. There is nothing to join. Yes, and that's fine, that's good in fact. (July 2009)

Introduction

Setting out a new theory of education is complex. This is compounded if the terrain offered involves restructuring how we commonly see education *and* is a shifting terrain open to iterability (repeatable in different contexts, each time with potential differences). The theory presented here is not one of learning but one of understanding education.

In the previous chapter contextual issues around EHE discovery and its implications have been considered. Before moving in Chapter Five, to the empirical data of the 'discovery moment' showing signs of paradigmatic diversity in educational studies at a structural level, it is necessary to build first a theoretical picture. The current chapter looks at what that data can mean and why. It looks at the personal nature and powerful difficulty of discovering educational difference – why it is not as simple as pressing a button and 'switching sides'. This is done from a perspective of incommensurability, interior tipping points, individual readiness and a desire for another, inchoate and emergent way forward. Except, that is, for the discovery 'moment', which serves as an *éclat*.

It is being suggested that this moment is the sign around which we can look at restructuring our current understanding of education. If we presently cannot conceive of education as being *necessarily* restructured, this is not exactly the issue. Alternative structures are potentially necessary in ways currently unconceived; just as scientific theories that are as yet beyond the scope of thought might one day prove valuable:

> ... even the most genuinely impressive and instrumentally accomplished theories of contemporary science will ultimately be replaced by more powerful conceptual tools offering fundamentally different conceptions of nature that have presently not yet even been conceived. (Stanford, 2006, p 211)

The sign of the moment of gestalt switching from one educational world to another that is seen in the data of this book, is an indication presented that we can conceive of education differently. To scaffold such a claim, Thomas Kuhn's scientific theory of discovery in the natural sciences is helpful. Furthermore I present Foucault's interest in socially and personally relevant care of the self, to show why a theory of discovery in and of education makes educationally oriented (rather than merely scientifically inclined) sense.

Deep need for discovery

The depth of the need to discover another educational pathway can be highlighted as something akin to requiring or acquiring a vocation. First generation adult home educators (those who themselves went to school)[1] on discovering the difference of EHE can experience it as a calling. As Hase and Kenyon mention with regard to personal changes, there are psychological features involved (Hase and Kenyon, 2007). Change from one educational pathway to another – where difference is involved – is most likely a sought solution to pain, discomfort or disappointment of some formative kind: 'people only change in response to a very clear need. This usually involves distress such as confusion, dissonance, and fear or a more positive motive such as intense desire' (Hase and Kenyon, 2007, p 112). EHE practice requires and involves personal change (Neuman and Avriam, 2003). Whatever the motivation for change it is an intensely experienced drive; not an easy option.

Biesta points to the location of a switch and a shift of paradigm as part of changes in consciousness. For another educational vision to be appreciated, significant movement of self is likely:

> ... our intuitions and convictions about education are not as 'natural' (and therefore inevitable) as they seem to be, but are closely related with the paradigm of the philosophy of consciousness. Given this, practical intersubjectivity requires

> a 'gestalt switch' and even entails – so it might be argued –
> something like a paradigm shift. (Biesta, 1994, p 317)

Not everyone, in other words, is called to discover home education in a genuine, deep-seated and meaningful manner. For those who are, the journey has no real signposts to follow. Intuition and personal conviction about what is right for them and their children lead the way. Philosophy plays a big part because no 'guide books' or 'information packs' about the impact and significance of discovery by adults new to home education exist. Given the very personal nature of the experience – as I will discuss below – neither should they, perhaps.

In such a sense, what I outline below then is bricolage (Kincheloe, 2001) to open and shine light on a situation: 'to discover what each of them could "signify"' (Levi-Strauss, 1966, p 18). It need not be seen as the definitive answer or framework of understanding. This theoretical assemblage here hopefully leaves such dogmatism behind. The connotation of bricolage as part of repairing something is particularly apt in the present context. The theory used in this text is employed towards creation of something that is reparative: where previously there was no theory or vision of how to understand the difference and self-styled narratives of the alternative paradigm of education, a bricolage of theories chosen for their explanatory powers and appropriateness can fill, or repair the situation.

Introduction to theory of difference in education

> Why not just take your kids out of school and teach them
> at home? (Holt, 2003, p 7)

As we can see from the above quote, home educating decisions are not rocket science. Recourse to practicalities as much as common sense, abide and have power. Yet, this simplicity belies a raft of philosophical underpinnings allowing, impacting and determining the education that occurs.

What kind of educational philosophy is involved in EHE? This is such a new area we can bricolage on new terms: in new ways, for contemporary, emergent reasons and using whatever resources work. However, a certain type of international philosophical background to EHE is found in historical accounts of how it has emerged as an alternative educational practice. Following on from a rich history of progressive education (Skidelsky, 1969; Röhrs and Lenhart, 1995), EHE accounts involving forms of philosophising are mostly found in books written in the last 30 years by advocates such as John Holt, from the US or Roland Meighan, based in England (Holt, 1977; Meighan, 1992; Holt, 2003). They are offered as what I would call, without denigration, 'home-spun' philosophical accounts: developing philosophical ideas but not within a dedicated academic philosophy of education arena.

Dedicated theoretical/philosophical work is still to be substantially achieved, although work begins to emerge (for example Davies, 2009; Merry and Howell, 2009; Lees, 2011a; McAvoy, 2012; Thomas and Pattison, 2013). Very few people have considered what a theory or philosophy of EHE might look like: there has been little direct *philosophical* (only) analysis of EHE involving its metaphysical, transcendental, existential, postmodern or any other philosophically involved elements. This raises questions such as: is philosophy of EHE possible? Is it different from philosophy dealing with mainstream schooling education? If it is, how? Philosophy has not yet been *applied* much to EHE, to understand it better. There is also a gap in our understanding of the similarities (and possible dissimilarities) of a philosophical kind, between EHE and democratic education practice, apart from other areas (see Chapter Three for discussion of communalities).

Of mainstreamed democratic educational theory there is a great deal, ranging from discussions of Ivan Illich (for example Bruno-Jofré and Zaldívar, 2012) to Paolo Freirean mutations on a theme (Roberts, 2012) and wider discussions (for example Friedrich et al, 2010). Of alternative democratic heutagogy in educational theory there is again, little, but more than with EHE because of links to famous schools such as Summerhill and no doubt the fact of this practice occurring in the familiar conceptual setting of a school (for example Hase and Kenyon, 2007; Stronach and Piper, 2008; Fielding, 2013). Histories of EHE which might trace philosophical developments are rare, although there are a few exceptions (Carper, 1992; Knowles et al, 1992; Carper, 2000; Gaither, 2008). Despite a significant body of varied empirical academic research done on EHE,[2] this literature focuses mostly on pedagogic, social and political issues, bringing philosophical considerations in only marginally.

More writings on EHE are proliferating (such as this book for instance) with the continuing global-wide rise in EHE numbers (especially in the US). An interest and a market emerge to know more about EHE and stimulate debate. Naturally, publications meet demand. Curricular materials form a significant publications sector, largely serving religiously oriented home educators whose practice is less autonomous (Stevens, 2003a). Yet, perhaps the philosophical elements in much of the outputs remains underdeveloped or if not can it utilise a standard philosophical canon? I suggest that the philosophical resources suited to EHE are unusual and unforeseeable. Why would this be? The 'canon' is *other* and emergent, not curricular. It is always open to fast-paced renegotiation and disavowal.

Feminist work has called for new forms of language and writing to underpin what is true to women's thought (for example Spender, 1980; Belenky et al, 1997), pointing out silences stemming from de-validation of other languages of knowing from the (patriarchal) hegemonic stance (Glenn, 2004). In similar ways, it is right to question whether the forms of philosophising, theorising and presentation which educational alternatives – as marginalised practice – offer, or would like for themselves, would be valid or acceptable according to current philosophy of education 'standards'. Current educational philosophy is conducted through conversations lacking reference to the deep *otherness* of EHE and other alternatives (Lees, 2011b; Safran, 2012). It has a bias to mainstream assumptions of the educational, functioning through languages of mainstream education that on EHE terms might not apply (Lees, 2012; Thomas and Pattison, 2013).

On their own terms alternatives may manifest in quite different ways from so far established naming, theorising and dynamics of knowing in educational philosophy. Women's work in philosophy shows the voids education allows without self-guilt; by not questioning what is missing (Roland Martin, 2003). EHE is in a similar situation of needing problematisation of such spaces and silences.

Creation of philosophy of EHE?

If it is not home-spun, historically or socially inclined and is instead philosophical, what applies? Which voices resonate? It is worth bearing in mind at this point that progressive education itself, as a broader church, has never really been able to fundamentally assert its own philosophy. John Dewey and his associates in the Progressive Education Association failed to 'agree on a consistent philosophy of progressive education' (New and Cochrane, 2007, p 668). Dewey wrote *Need for a philosophy of education* (Dewey, 1964) to address the issue of progressive education having to have 'its own foundation and frame' (Doll, 1993, p 182). Whether this has ever been achieved presently remains a moot point. A substantial problem might well be a lack of definition:

> Progressive education is not indeed a term susceptible of
> exact delimitation. Hopes of anything approaching a reliable

definition have been adamantly dashed by one of the
knowledgeable experts in this field, Lawrence A. Cremin:
'none exists,' he tells us, 'and none ever will'. (Röhrs and
Lenhart, 1995, p 11)

But this also might be a starting point.

Returning to our focus on EHE, it is suggested from nascent
investigations of a philosophical kind into this area, that its philosophical
basis is far from the Anglo–American analytical tradition. Instead,
a Continental philosophical outlook offers promise. Theoretical
conditions of postmodernism such as openness or incredulity towards
'metanarratives' (Lyotard, 1984) are in tune with the practices of EHE.
There seems no reason also why developments in thought such as
complexity theory and even quantum theory (see for example Capra,
1975), cannot have much to say to help philosophise and illuminate
EHE as a specific educational modality of interest both to itself and to
mainstream educational theory, practice and research.

Attention and an imperative, even, for developing a robust philosophy
of education that is right for EHE practice is ongoing. In the Education
Committee session cited also previously, discussion highlights a lack in
this regard useful to fill. As an example of a gap in needful conversations,
the exchange below is indicative of much causing difficulties for
EHE as education. EHE lacks integrated theory open to discursive
understanding:

> **Q260 Chair:** Do you have a philosophical objection to state
> funding support for those who make this choice? It is the
> parent's duty to ensure the education of their child; they
> can delegate it to the state, for which the state then pays.
> If they choose to take what the Government and you
> suggest is a perfectly valid decision to provide education
> themselves, do you have a philosophical objection to the
> state providing additional financial support to supplement
> that of the parents?
>
> **Elizabeth Truss:** No, I do not, is the answer.
>
> **Q261 Chair:** So it is primarily about resources and the rest
> of it.
>
> **Elizabeth Truss:** I think so. I have not given a great deal of
> thought to philosophy since I have joined the Department
> for Education, because I am focused on the various issues
> in hand. I will certainly consider my philosophical views,
> particularly after I have read the report.

Chair: Excellent. Well, I hope your personal dialectic will allow you to come to the right conclusions.

Q262 Ian Mearns: How would you treat an application from, say, 150 home educators in Norfolk to establish a virtual free school?

Elizabeth Truss: When you talk about home educators, my understanding is those children would be educated at home, which is a different concept from a school, so I am not sure exactly how that would work. I do not know, is the honest answer.

Q263 Ian Mearns: Home educators in my borough of Gateshead all do it very differently. Some of them engage tutors and they have sessions in the library and they go to other places, so the possibility of a virtual free school, which would employ teaching staff or tutors, is not beyond the realms of possibility, is it?

Elizabeth Truss: Well, we are into the question of when is a school not a school, I suppose.

Chair: Back to philosophy.

Elizabeth Truss: We are back to philosophy. It is a very philosophical session at this Committee.

Chair: Less avoidable than you thought.

Elizabeth Truss: I am in favour of philosophy, do not get me wrong. I would need to look at the terms and conditions of the free school proposal in more detail to see how that would work. Clearly, when you start talking about employing teachers and having lessons, it is becoming more of a school and less of a home education experience, I might suggest. But there is obviously a continuum and, in life, some things just do not fit into boxes.

(House of Commons Education Committee, 2012, p Ev 36)

Philosophy of EHE was also evident in the deliberations around the 2009 Badman Review discussed in the previous chapter. There was philosophically inclined debate on a number of issues: the terms, in law, of a 'suitable and efficient' education (Badman, 2009, p 55); EHE as an educational modality requiring or denying monitoring; the status of autonomous education within EHE and education more broadly; the outcomes for the self of EHE; how EHE outcomes relate to citizenship; how EHE families relate to the concept of community; the status of EHE as a product of self-removal from a 'mainstream', and so on.

Those who think dealing with EHE is a simple matter of decisions and policies, come up against the fact that it is located at the heart of educational philosophy. They emerge from simplistic assumptions bruised by this fact. Perhaps they are also surprised by the complexity of the issues, entwined as they are in and with what education, in whatever mode of practice, *means.*

Should we care if there are no concerted attempts to philosophise EHE? Philosophical content would entail having '*entwicklungsfähigkeit*' (developmental capability: author's translation) which is, in Giorgio Agamben's mind (quoting from Feuerbach), the best possible definition of philosophy that we can hope for (Agamben, 2002). Agamben states:

> If a work, be it a work of art, or science, or scholarship, has some value then it will contain this philosophical element. Something which has remained unsaid in it and demands to be unfolded and worked out. (Agamben, 2002)

So EHE research and writing without saying the unsaid; or unfolding the knowledge to-come is less valuable? Agamben's idea of philosophy applied to EHE highlights how our concept of it is still in its earliest stages. Present scenarios bear this out. As mentioned previously with regard to educationism against EHE, there are high levels of conceptual ignorance which abound in response to EHE realities: what Graham Stuart MP called 'commonly held ignorant attitudes' (House of Commons Education Committee, 2012, p Ev 18). These need conceptual development belonging to a philosophical remit. This is not work to be dismissed either. Lest we forget: conceptual ignorance of EHE from those in authority has resulted in parents having their children removed from their care and a number of other serious difficulties causing stress and concern.

Ignorance is not just within local authority education departments. It is rife in social services. A prospective adopter in 2010, wishing to suggest EHE *might* be a positive approach for an adopted child was told – without any knowledge of EHE as educational practice on the part of the adoption social worker – that such a scenario is 'abusive' and 'neglectful' because it denies a child schooling. This is a ridiculous statement based on a lack of knowledge of EHE practice involving autonomy and choice for the child, which could include school attendance but might not. I have heard anecdotally from a former senior social worker that *most* social workers view EHE with great suspicion as a *serious* potential safeguarding issue. EHE needs philosophical improvements and greater support from theory so that the influential opinions of social workers in deciding child placements and even removals can be made more informed and balanced. Appropriate theory can inform social work training for the sake of all who come into contact with social workers.

Clearly appreciating what EHE is, how it functions and how it might be the best educational option for particular children is vitally important. In a democratic society premised on the belief that we seek not to cause harm through racism, sexism, prejudice and other bad attitudes, having an appropriate attitude to EHE is an imperative in some instances. This makes its case as subject to 'educationism' an unusual one for educational studies. Better theory underpins *justice* for this educational modality and its potential for children.

The gateless gate of home education discovery

So, there is much of philosophical intrigue surrounding EHE. An approach is now offered that seems to fit well with the idea of EHE as non-binary and involving 'mystery' and its discovery being full of chance and challenge. The idea of the 'gateless gate' comes from Zen philosophical koan-style thought.

The seemingly nonsensical phrase of a gateless gate symbolises and describes how discovery occurs in real terms. It offers an understanding of the philosophy that underpins genuine discovery in a way that can then lead to EHE practice being educationally fruitful:

> The great path has no gates,
> Thousands of roads enter it.
> When one passes through this gateless gate
> He (sic) walks freely between heaven and earth. (Reps, 2000, p 114)

> Joshu asked Nansen: What is the path?
> Nansen said: Everyday life is the path.
> Joshu asked: Can it be studied?
> Nansen said: If you try to study, you will be far away from it.
> Joshu asked: If I do not study, how can I know it is the path?
> Nansen said: The path does not belong to the perception world, neither does it belong to the nonperception world.
> Cognition is a delusion and noncognition is senseless.
> If you want to reach the true path beyond doubt, place

yourself in the same freedom as sky. You name it neither
good nor not-good.
At these words Joshu was enlightened. (Reps, 2000,
p 134)

Home education is not a set practice. It is emergent, made up,
spontaneous, free. Koans are a kind of metaphorical style tale pointing
obliquely to a truth and the ones quoted above suggest that an
alternative framework of cognition than a linear logic can apply to
understanding something. In the present case, the discovery of EHE
(and other alternatives) does not lend itself to logical understandings.
How to plan for coming upon EHE with an open mind? How to
predict the causes of interest? This is impossible other than noting
possible prior problems with schooling that might predispose a parent
to seek for an alternative pathway.

Rather than a Cartesian, rational and binary approach of a 'mechanistic
view of life' – similar to Newtonian physics in structure – (Capra, 1983)
and involving ideas of measurement and assessment, discovery of EHE
(etc) is a 'happening' or 'event' in the personal. Each case is unique to
the individual and their moment and circumstances of discovery. There
are no set relations to expose and follow. It is an opening and a flight
into 'rhizomatic' freedoms 'enabling one to blow apart strata, cut roots
and make new connections' (Deleuze and Guattari, 2004, p 16).

The gateless gate theory of EHE discovery is therefore – aptly – an
issue of some complexity. The kinds of theories being now applied to
education emerging from scientific complexity theory, fit the gateless
gate of EHE discovery (and always implied in such discovery is that of
other alternatives such as democratic schooling). Complexity theorising
for education includes emergent selves (Osberg et al, 2008), alternative
epistemologies (Biesta and Osberg, 2007; Osberg and Biesta, 2007),
merging theories and simultaneities (Davis, 2008) and postmodern
perspectives on the curriculum (Doll, 1993). This can be seen through
an educational lens, as part of the dissolution of the binary of school
and not-school.

Zen philosophical ideas such as 'mu' and 'nothing' (Watts, 1974)
resonate in the domain being sketched of philosophies appropriate to
EHE. Zen philosophy 'fits' into the postmodern perspective (Olsen,
2000), mentioned above, as part of a deconstructive scene responsive to
EHE discovery. However the whole point is that nothing is expected
or anticipated to *fit*. This is how people end up discovering alternative
education as something that attracts them; that they wish to investigate
further with a view to pursuing it. A new 'fit' that does not, this time,

constrain; a nothing in the place of something and a negation of what was previously sure but became a disappointment.

Thus, the most valid theory of the discovery of EHE is possibly a meta-theory of 'non-theory'. Nevertheless there are theoretical frames which have shown themselves to be particularly appropriate and useful. As previously mentioned, these are Kuhn's philosophy of the structure of scientific revolutions (1962) and Foucault's late philosophy of an ethical art of the self (1986). There are certainly other frameworks of use, but I found these two to work wonderfully to better understand discovery. A further theory of relevance to what occurs prior to discovery is Hirschman's theory of exit, voice and loyalty (Hirschman, 1970), discussed in Chapter Seven.

Kuhnian significance

Thomas S. Kuhn's philosophy of scientific discovery has relevance for this book's discussion of EHE discovery. I also place Kuhn's relevance at the heart of why EHE is important for educational studies as a whole. A small moment in the life of a scientist can revolutionise scientific understanding and eventually even society. A small moment in the lives of ordinary people has the power to change the face of education.

Kuhn presented paradigms as a function of understanding: they are at the heart of the operationalisation of knowledge. That is an idea borne out by Giorgio Agamben's recognition of the French historian of Greek philosophy Victor Goldschmidt's interest in paradigms: 'the analysis of an apparently minor problem such as the paradigm sheds a completely new light on the whole of Plato's philosophy' (Agamben, 2002). It is then no surprise that Kuhnian paradigmatic philosophy should surface in a study claiming to be at the heart of the operationalisation of knowledge in education.

Kuhn's work on paradigms has itself been far reaching in influence (Bird, 2000). If the gestalt switch moment and paradigm shifting of the participants in this study shown in the stories included in the next chapter can have importance for education, this is a feature of paradigm recognition as a powerful changer of perceptions. Theoretical discussion of this empirical data may – as a paradigmatic function in action – be able to affect the future (and history) of education as we see it. This would be then because, following Agamben again, 'what makes something intelligible is the paradigmatic exhibition of its own knowability' (2002).

What is a paradigm?

The term paradigm is presented here as a concept roughly analogous to some of Kuhn's meanings outlined below. This word has a history of explication (Mey, 1992) under different conditions (Fleck, 1935; Conant, 1951). This includes its use by Wittgenstein as a model or stereotype (Preston, 2008, p 22). Since Kuhn published *The structure of scientific revolutions* in 1962, 'paradigm' has been a concept of significant contemporary mainstream consideration and importance for science; also in areas outside of natural science's defining interests. Yet, a definitive answer to the question, 'what is a paradigm?' remains somewhere on the level of Margaret Masterman's identification of 21 separate uses of the term paradigm by Kuhn in *Structure* (Masterman, 1970). Giorgio Agamben attempts an analysis in his lecture 'What is a paradigm?' (2009). In tune with the gateless gate koan theory of this book, what Agamben does in that lecture is to open up understanding of the paradigm to koan-type thought, exemplified in the lines he quotes from a poem by Wallace Stevens, *Description without place*: 'It is possible that to seem, it is to be. And the sun is something seeming, and it is. The sun is an example. What it seems, it is. And in such seeming all things are'.

Diffusiveness around the meaning of a paradigm is perhaps appropriate in a postmodern age, but a rough working definition can be sketched. This is done here following Kuhn, whose conception of paradigms was called by Foucault as 'admirable and definitive' (Agamben, 2009, p 10). Kuhn's vision suggests a paradigm is an area of enquiry with epistemological boundaries that can be breached. Boundary crossing leads to the creation of new paradigms with different areas and even new rules of enquiry. New foci and directions of thought take over from their predecessor claims of validity and research attention. Specifically Kuhn highlighted two types of paradigm: 'exemplars' as units of excellence to teach; and the wider, famous meaning of a paradigm as a 'disciplinary matrix' (Kuhn, 1962). This is 'the entire constellation of beliefs, values, techniques and so on shared by the members of a given [scientific] community' (Kuhn, 1962, p 175).

The nature of a paradigm as existing at all is of utmost importance for the location of the current focus of an enquiry concerning the found phenomenon, or otherwise, of a 'gestalt switch' or 'conversion' between a schooling mentality and a belief in another world and way of education. EHE, *discovered*, is found as something 'special'. Kuhn's presentation of paradigms is his own. Not everyone agrees he has the right formula (see Preston, 2008, for an overview of commentators and Bird, 2000, for an in-depth analysis of Kuhn's work). But, in this present text, his theoretical framework is largely accepted as valid and valuable for the arguments presented. The nature of a paradigm as containing crisis, conversion, competition, incommensurability and community are discussed by Kuhn, in a way that very closely corresponds to what the data shows. It fits and explains events in the social sciences (see Bird, 2000) as well as the natural sciences, offering avenues for discussion. Kuhn wrote that 'it remains an open question what parts of social science have yet acquired such paradigms at all' (1962, p 15). I am suggesting education is paradigmatic in a Kuhnian sense (at a deep structural, modality level) because the data presented fits this idea; indeed signifies this possibility.

So, for present purposes, a paradigm as a community of investigators considering how a domain of inquiry can be developed; the community itself is a product of revolutionary ideas emerging from a period of crisis. One or more people noticed anomalies in a situation and sought for answers. The solution became common to those seekers and this formed a community of believers in a new 'way'; a way that was a solution to the problem of the crisis of anomalies. At this juncture we need to question why the identification of a 'gestalt switch' mechanism might be so important for a discipline to obtain a paradigmatic identity.

What is a gestalt switch?

Gestalt switch, as a term used by Kuhn, is a phrase that signifies a turn or change of the whole (gestalt). It is a switch in allegiance between or focus on differing paradigms or 'shifts in perception' of cognitive data (Kuhn, 1962, p 113). Kuhn also used the phrase 'world changes'. In Kuhn's taxonomy it is a form of revolution: 'scientific development also displays a noncumulative mode' (Kuhn, 2000b); happening in a 'relatively sudden' way (Kuhn, 2000b, pp 122, 150), although there may have been a long lead up to the moment where the change occurs:

> But after the subject has begun to learn to deal with [her/] his new world, [her/]his entire visual field flips over, usually after an intervening period in which vision is simply confused (p 112).

To judge whether this change has indeed occurred or not 'we must look for indirect and behavioural evidence that the scientist with a new paradigm sees differently from the way [she/]he had seen before' (p 115). The 'transformations of vision' (p 118) that are involved are internal to the human as a private experience. Affects on thinking and language occur:

> revolutionary changes are ... problematic. They involve discoveries that cannot be accommodated within the concepts in use before they were made. In order to make or to assimilate such a discovery one must alter the way one thinks about and describes some range of natural phenomenon. (Kuhn, 2000b, p 14–15)

A description by Kuhn of a gestalt switch in action, recorded as a memory of the time of its happening, is the following:

> Suddenly the fragments in my head sorted themselves out in a new way, and fell into place together. My jaw dropped, for all at once Aristotle seemed a very good physicist indeed, but of a sort I'd never dreamed possible. (p 16)

A gestalt switch involves realisation:

> ... the central change cannot be experienced piecemeal, one step at a time. Instead it involves some relatively sudden and unstructured transformation in which some part of the flux of experience sorts itself out differently and displays patterns that were not visible before. (p 17)

This has implications for the claim of this book that EHE is a (newly but increasingly recognised) *paradigm* of education (see Miller, 2008; Mintz and Ricci, 2010). It is not just a mini-phenomenon of rising numbers or a modern lifestyle choice, but a structural challenge. The problematisation involves the nature, conduct, assumptions, epistemology and ontology of educational studies: if it is true that it is underpinned too concretely by one conventional model this will change. If EHE can show some facility to challenge educational studies' conventional hegemony in a paradigmatic manner of discovery of a new paradigm, then challenges to this hegemony and dominance are potentially open to success. For instance, calls for more democracy in schools might be furnished with some epistemological support for challenge to ossified attitudes. Difficulties with stubborn lack of change to educational practices, where democracy is too slow to embed coherently (see for example Harber and Mncube, 2012; 2013), might be overcome with paradigm shift behaviour. This can be organised through community action and active refutation of old behaviours. If the nature of the field is open to shifts, the dominance of non-democratic schooling is ultimately escapable. Unfortunately perhaps, Kuhn highlights that the old guard need to fade out; they will not surrender and are unlikely to change their minds (Kuhn, 1962).

Change is cataclysmic for the old guard due to sudden transformation that cannot be returned to an old order, so what follows in the present context of discussion is change in education. Expecting equality of treatment of EHE and alternatives as a domain/s of education in its/ their own right, amongst other domains of education, becomes more feasible. A shift from educational marginality to *difference* occurs. All paradigms of education are technically *equal* as paradigms at least, despite resource and population differences. For paradigms to be recognised as equal in this way, signs of a gestalt switch into EHE are key because this suggests the nature of the territory as paradigmatic at a structural level. However, paradigmatic 'equality' requires a 'level playing field' where value given to paradigms is not hierarchically determined.

That the change can be structural is interesting. The social sciences have power to affect *being* and *becoming* when their theoretical and practical lenses change. Huge implications follow from structural shifts. In the natural sciences the Copernican revolution is an impactful example. Seeing through education differently can change the society, politics, economics and international outcomes of nation states.

In the empirical data in Chapter Five, strong indications of a gestalt switch occurring between different structures of education are shown: in the form of comments about 'shifts,' 'clicks' and sudden realisations bringing a change from a conception of education as schooling to an understanding of a way in which education can happen in an entirely different mode. These shifts happen across a level terrain.

Kuhnian revolution of self

Kuhn suggests that when differing groups of scientists are located in two different 'worlds' (as in paradigms) they 'see different things when they look from the same point in the same direction' (Kuhn, 1962, p 150). Furthermore, although the onlooker is 'confronting the same constellation of objects as before and knowing that [she/]he does so, [she/]he nevertheless finds them transformed through and through in many of their details' (p 122). Moreover Kuhn goes so far as to suggest that in fact the world that was there before the gestalt switch no longer exists: 'The data themselves had changed. That is the last of the senses in which we may want to say that after a revolution scientists work in a different world' (p 135).

We therefore have in the concept of a gestalt switch a radical transformation of perception and being. This is intriguing. Gestalt switches in the Kuhnian sense are something which are as yet under-researched. Even in Bird's exhaustive study of Kuhnian thought, gestalt switches receive scant attention (2000). They are not well understood. Presently they feature more in the domain of cognitive science research for example, rather than being used to make sense of social science reports of changes in behaviours and perceptions. The idea of switching has been utilised for the purposes of artificial intelligence developments (Mey, 1992). Awareness of the possibility of a gestalt switch mechanism, since Kuhn suggested that this was necessary for the conversion from one paradigm to another, has increased. We are still at the beginning of our understanding of the 'cognitive mechanism' of gestalt switches and the nature and reasons for their occurrence.

'Gestalt switch' used by Kuhn in the context of scientific discoveries may be one way to say something which other domains express differently. Religious discourse speaks of conversion experiences (Chester, 2003). A modern version of gestalt switch might be the use of the term 'Aha!' (George, 2008). Popularisation of the idea of 'switching' seems to be gaining momentum, spurred on by technology (Bartscherer and Coover, 2011). Noticing a gestalt switch is to find paradigms functioning. It is like discovering the existence of a new planet.

Paradigms in education

Usually in education, 'paradigms' are discussed as being worlds within education as conflated with schooling; for example the mini-paradigm of accountability (Stickney, 2006), various theoretical approaches to research methodology (Guba, 1990; Donmoyer, 1996) or paradigms of policy and politics (Mehta, 2013). As Mehta suggests: 'Scholars of paradigm changes should recognize that "paradigms create politics" as well' (Mehta, 2013, p 293). I could not agree more, as what follows in coming chapters highlights. Unlike the mini-paradigms just alluded to however, I move the boundaries away from the confines of the school *as* education; thereby *repositioning* the school through a new vision of how paradigms function in education; changing the political landscape of education as a whole territory (not schooling *per se*); making it *flat*.

It is being suggested here that education *without schools* is an emergent paradigm of education in another sense than as a mini-paradigm: it is a deep challenge to the structure of paradigms of education (that are actually currently not of education, but of the school) just mentioned. Schooling-oriented mini-paradigms will never impact upon the grammar of schooling (Tyack and Cuban, 1995) but structural paradigm wars can. Education is not a field of mini-paradigms of schooling, with alternatives as one of those mini-elements. It is a field wherein schooling is one paradigm and education *without* schools is another. They sit side by side as equal, not one within the other. This changes the nature of education.

After a structural shift where education *without* schools is also education *proper*, education *with* schools shows itself up as overblown in its importance educationally speaking. It cannot claim structural dominance and 'high ground' even if it can claim resources and attendance/involvement dominance, being just one option in the educationally *flat* landscape. Suddenly the power of education *as* schooling is lessened. Schooling is an *option*, not education. Such a way of seeing education afresh overturns the present structures of educational studies, highlighting ignorance about education. There is an assumption of the dominance of the school as education. The data from the study showing switching behaviour highlights a new model is required: a structurally level multi-paradigmatic model.

We can see things differently. A fresh perspective has education as the home of a powerful and dominant 'mega-paradigm' which is schooling and its mentality, touching all education perhaps through its tentacled reach. *But this is no longer conflated with education.* Previously the conflation of education with schooling allowed only for an epistemological structure that was top-down or enclosed: education as *schooling* at the top and beneath or within this 'mega' paradigm lay the various inner, minor/mini-paradigms such as narratives, qualitative/ quantitative research methodologies, postmodernism etc. EHE and democratic schooling were also seen as within this mega-paradigm; often as somewhere 'low-down'. Because all of education was located in this mega-paradigm of schooling, it becomes the field itself.

The emergence of EHE and democratic schooling as within an alternative paradigm of education is a revolution. Education is now two worlds: schooling and alternatives to schooling, side by side. Just as with schooling, within alternatives are various mini-worlds, one of which is EHE and within EHE are various mini-worlds such as conservative Christian approaches (Kunzman, 2009) and autonomous approaches (Thomas and Pattison, 2007; Bergeron, 2009). Then, of course within both paradigms of schooling and alternatives are distinct paradigms of theory or practice. The change this level perspective offers is that schooling no longer dominates our understanding *as* education.

When it comes to the assessment of the various paradigms of education, schooling, in this text, is considered as a failed (or failing) paradigm of education. It acts outside of its nature (which, as shown here, is paradigmatic) by acting as if it is education itself as a field. This has significant negative consequences for the ability of schooling to do what Kuhn would call 'normal science' in creating development of the paradigm. The new structure for educational studies advocated, confers upon such schooling, as a *mere* paradigm of education, a role in the life of the human that deserves substantial scrutiny and challenge for being outside of its capacity and remit: for being megalomaniacal. This is fully in line with trenchant criticisms of schooling as education having become a foreclosing, governmental technology (Flint and Peim, 2012). In other words, schooling needs to wake up to the competition and 'step down' with humility. Step down from expecting and perpetuating '… the overwhelming emphasis on schools and teachers …' in educational work (Suissa, 2006, p 66).

But there is no getting away from the size and power of schooling. In being, however, a 'mega-paradigm' of education (now not *the* paradigm but the largest and currently most influential in terms of concept creation), schooling has a responsibility. This is an educational responsibility to acknowledge its position (as hegemonic); to develop what Bernstein calls the requirement of 'the cultivation of hermeneutical sensitivity and imagination' (Bernstein, 1991, p 92). A sensitivity of respect for a less powerful and less well-resourced paradigm of education such as alternatives to school attendance, including EHE – rather than condemnation and dismissal – is appropriate. This is especially needed in the face of paradigmatic difference. Kuhn's attendant concept of incommensurability identifies a need for sensitive understandings of difference in order to avoid intolerance, persecution and miscomprehension (Kuhn, 2000a).

For Kuhn a key lasting problematic for his presentation of paradigmatic revolutions was the issue of incommensurability (Kuhn, 2000a). This is the impossibility of communication between people located in different paradigms: although they refer to the same thing and seem to use the same language, their meanings are totally different due to the nature of their differing world views. Thus, they talk at cross-purposes. As previously mentioned educational alternatives have grappled with incommensurability issues: people who just don't 'get' what EHE and democratic schooling have to offer on their own terms and therefore challenge their validity as good education practice (see Chapter Three). Within the data in the next chapter (and in Chapter Two), there is plenty to indicate that incommensurability is a problem.

People either side of the 'divide' find it hard to communicate in ways convincing to others outside of the 'circle of conversion', who cannot understand why EHE practices work and how or why EHE ought to be believed in so vehemently, because they quite literally do not see from that point of view.

Discovery of what?

When individuals discover EHE they report new effects on the self (see data in Chapter Five). Strikingly, these effects, their rationale for being *allowed* into the self and the philosophical framework within which they sit, all match closely the later work of Michel Foucault on technologies and care of the self. This work by Foucault has been widely seen as a 'turn' away from his previous concerns (Foucault, 1993): a radical break with the interests he had before, in aspects of power and social relationships within a constructed framework of controls, towards a deep interest in ethical agency.

Power and social relationships are important parts of EHE discovery, research literature and practice concerns. However, I would like to focus on something that I think is fairly new with regards to our understanding of what EHE is about. As education EHE is a *self-discovery journey* for adults (and children). Either educationally, socially or politically it causes learning and curiosity. It is existential and intimate – personally affecting as an education mode (see for example McKee, 2002).

If EHE as a feature of a person's life (most adults discovering EHE went to school because this is, after all, the hegemonic norm which only recently developed its numbers) returns a person to their own sense of self and well-being; indeed to heightened happiness – what has a mainstream educational heritage achieved? This has implications for what education, as it currently hegemonically functions in the mainstream, *does* to people. Does it shut them down? Hide themselves from themselves? Distance people from their true being? Are we making a terrible mistake with current mainstream education because of what it does – and does not do – to and for people? There is a great deal of alternative educational literature focusing on the toxic effects of mainstream schooling to support such questioning (for example Meighan, 2004; Harber, 2009b; Olson, 2009).

Foucault as a theorist relevant to EHE

Foucault approached his ethical 'turn,' as a newly discovered topic of care and ethics of the self (Foucault, 1983a; Foucault, 1983b; Foucault, 1986; Foucault, 1988c). It is interesting to note that this work possibly follows an appreciative reading of Dewey's democratic educational approach (Auxier, 2002), as well as other writers on education such as Degérando, who featured on Foucault's radar (see Foucault, 2002, pp 72 and 261), and who spoke about 'care of the self': 'the life of man is in reality but one continued education, the end of which is to make himself perfect' (Degérando, 1830, p 24). This community of others who had written on care of the self includes Jan Patočka who wrote on Greek philosophy and published a book entitled 'care of the soul', of which Foucault was aware (Szakolczai, 1994). Technologies of care for the self are not a new topic from Foucault onwards.

From ancient times, caring for one's being has been a topic of interest to humans. What is particular perhaps – for the present discussion – about Foucault's focus on this subject, is in its exactitude of match to the notion of the discovery of EHE in a particular combination of elements. Also of note is the extent to which it seems to possibly draw its philosophical materials from educational thought. Foucault's notion of 'care of the self' is spiritual without being linked to any creed (Foucault, 1983a). EHE discovery is not a belief in a religion but a belief in a self that is 'sacred' to its own existence (Chapter Five). The 'arts of existence' which Foucault discusses, such as writing in a journal (Foucault, 1986), are used as directed but emergent tools of self-formation to 'craft' the subject (Butler, 2005). This happens in the same way that a pedagogical/heutagogical framework involving volitional structures of autonomous education forms the self: to exist well, but here through *unstructured* educational engagement dependent on volition (Neill, 1968; D'Marea Bassett, 2008). This occurs in the same way as choosing to write in a journal, which is a volitional act of freedom where structures of meaning evolve *because* of freedom.

Furthermore, Foucault's conceptualisation of the purpose of these 'arts' is not to fit in and be accepted within a given world but rather to push the limits of that world, adopting a critical stance in order to find what else can be (Foucault, 1991; Healy, 2001). This is similar in attitude to the atmospheres of alternatives, which consider that the ways in which most children grow up according to mainstream schooling, and its side-effect of alienation from what is natural, ought to be challenged by both example and education towards adopting other attitudes (Llewellyn, 1993; Spring, 1998; Bergeron, 2009). How did Foucault construct this philosophy of the self and its formation?

Technologies of the self

Foucault understood that there are '"truth games" related to techniques that human beings use to understand themselves' (Foucault, 1988c, p 18). He delineated such techniques as different from other types of techniques: production, signs and power. The technologies of the self of which he spoke were to do with humans effecting:

> ... by their own means or with the help of others a certain number of operations on their own bodies and souls, thought, conduct, and way of being, so as to transform themselves in order to attain a certain state of happiness, purity, wisdom, perfection or immortality. (Foucault, 1988c, p 18)

Technologies of the self in ancient Greece – a focus of Foucault's conception of this phrasing – were about taking care of oneself: 'rules for social and personal conduct and for the art of life' (Foucault, 1988c, p 19). This is emphasised more than the maxim 'know thyself'. Of a different character, 'take care of oneself' is located within a paradigm of the emotions. 'Know thyself' is located in a source or target paradigm of cognition. Foucault suggests that technologies of the self, having more to do with caring rather than knowing, are to be privileged in an ethics he offers as new (Foucault, 1983b).

For our purposes here this has significant implications. It highlights a way of understanding EHE as a pedagogy/heutagogy (Thomas and Pattison, 2007) and fundamental lifestyle change (Neuman and Avriam, 2003) which looks upon care of the self as an instrument and teleology within education. Education becomes a way to care for the self, privileging this focus over and above learning for external ends such as test scores, university attendance or career triumph. In mainstream schooling a means–end mentality dominates (Peim and Flint, 2009). Even therapeutic education agendas of the school can be critically seen as managed instrumentally and without regard for self-autonomy (Ecclestone and Hayes, 2009). However, others disagree with this criticism, seeing the 'therapeutic turn' as 'a proper concern with the affective dimension of learning' (Hyland, 2011, p 3).

In terms of the educational atmosphere that best suits 'care of the self' developments, a pedagogic paradigm privileging freedom is required.

No other atmosphere is sufficiently flexible to accommodate the unique emergence of the individual (Biesta, 2006). As Foucault says: 'liberty is the ontological condition of ethics. But ethics is the deliberate form assumed by liberty' (Bernhauer and Rasmussen, 1988, p 4). If care of the self is an *ethical* project, one must be free. If care of the self is an *educational* project, one must be free.

Such atmospheres are found *a priori* in EHE of the autonomous form and democratic schools such as Summerhill. 'Care of the self' technologies introduced into mainstream schools suffer problems: they are not organised around fear-free truth telling and thus cannot accept the vicissitudes of human self-formation (Besley, 2007). Nor can the power of self-formation in terms of its fearlessness of the truth be accepted in educational scenarios where compromises are required due to management of large groups. Democracy of a deliberative kind becomes inconvenient at best (Olssen, 2007).

Thus, technologies of the self are *not* suited to mainstream schools. They are in fact antithetical to such education at a deep philosophical level of aims and purposes. Where they are suited is in an open-ended space of self and time, where interactions are facilitated and promoted 'so that man (sic) can be reconciled with himself' (Foucault, 1988b, p 2). Self possession is the means to control of one's environment, including interactions with others in an ethical manner (pp 7–8). Technologies of the self are the art of living ethically without having recourse to being told by another what to do so that ethical acts happen.

Care of the self and the discovery of EHE

Freedom is a key element in a Foucauldian exposition of ancient Greek practices of care of the self (Foucault, 2005), within which it can be seen also as its *necessary condition*: in being free from needing to work in the fields, or being overly concerned with affairs of state, for example. This corresponds with EHE experience where parents and children no longer have to negotiate the demands of the school day and the pressures that its timetable imposes. Discovering EHE is discovering freedom from such constraints and expectations.

Foucault mentions a specific effect on the self pertaining to care of the self practices relevant to EHE outcomes. This is *phusiologia*:

> *Phusiologia* gives the individual boldness and courage, a kind of intrepidity, which enables him (sic) to stand firm not only against the many beliefs that others wish to impose on him,

but also against life's dangers and the authority of those who
want to lay down the law. (Foucault, 2005, p 240)

Again, such effects on the self are seen in the research data in Chapter
Five, where discovering EHE is an entrance into a world which poses
challenges and difficulties as a little understood practice; requiring
practitioners to be bold in the face of the 'authority' of the Badman
Review, for example, or the prejudice of neighbours. Testimonies in
EHE stories and literature of such effects on the self of intrepidity as a
result of EHE and democratic alternative education practice abound
(Goodsman, 1992; Sheffer, 1995; Cameron and Meyer, 2006; Lees,
2008; Miller, 2008).

Another effect on the self developed through care of the self and
relating to EHE practice is *autarkeia*:

> ... the well known notion of *autarkeia*. That is to say, they
> will depend only on themselves. They will be *contenti*
> (content with themselves, satisfied with themselves). But ...
> they will need nothing other than themselves. However, at
> the same time, they will find a number of resources within
> themselves, and the possibility in particular of experiencing
> pleasure and delight in the full relationship they will have
> with themselves. (Foucault, 2005, p 241)

Again, discourse within alternative educational communities of such
effects on the self is common (Sheffer, 1995; Dowty, 2000; McKee,
2002). Children in an EHE paradigm of education report having
confidence and self-reliance (Llewellyn, 1993) and are noticed as being
self-poised (Meighan, 2005, p 27).

Schooling can hurt the self and its formation and EHE can heal
it (Sheffer, 1995; Wray and Thomas, 2013). Many of the research
interview participants voiced this feeling: the technologies of the self
evident in EHE had, to their minds, saved them. Whereas Michael
Apple discusses this 'saviour' effect as ideological and a form of social
divisiveness (Apple, 2000b), he fails to appreciate the cycle of despair
generated by schooling as an institutionalised system. The subsequent
joy on the part of those discovering EHE is a visceral and very real
personal event of great individual and family importance, as we will
see shortly in the data.

The otherness of the educational modality and situation discovered
in EHE instigates or causes a conversion *to* the self, involving: '... a real
shift, a certain movement of the subject with regard to [her/]himself'

(Foucault, 2001, pp 207–12). Foucault's joy in the idea of 'a certain determination to throw off familiar ways of thought and to look at the same things in a different way' (Foucault, 1988a, p 328) is found in escape into EHE. This is because it is sought for in response to a need for care of the self. That need is met by and is inherent in the special nature of the discovery outlined above with the gateless gate theory. No answer is given; people find their own way forward. This might be difficult but the way is surer; personalised; fitting.

A 'conversion to the self' is spoken of by Foucault as relating to the 'metaphor of navigation':

> ... in this idea of navigation, there is the theme that the port we are seeking is the homeport, the port in which we will find again our place of origin, our homeland. The path towards the self will always be something of an Odyssey. (Foucault, 2001, p 248)

With regard to EHE this is important because often remarks were made by participants in the research this book refers to about EHE as a journey that takes them to happiness.

The other aspect offered by techniques of the self is autonomous practice. Foucault was quite clear that this form of self 'stylisation' was a newly discovered way (albeit ancient) to ensure human autonomy in the face of domination. He understood that domination was not the first, nor the last, context for humans as they went about determining their own life. In a sense he indicated that care of the self was a secret and perhaps even surprisingly powerful way to truth about how humans develop; not in the face of domination and power but 'underground' as a vital and natural part of their interest in themselves (Foucault, 2000).

If this holds for EHE discovery it means that the marginality of discovery is in fact part of the attraction. Discoverers become special by being interested in something that is not mainstream and this outsider status enables them to effectively deal with domination. If then these educational worlds, as autonomous practices of the self, are discovered, does that mean that matrices of power are eluded? Are those powers which encompass the human, as per Foucault's earlier ideas on governmentality (Foucault, 1977), able to be circumvented through a modality of education with the power to change the self and the self's relationship to others?

Conclusion

How is discovery of an educational alternative possible if a concept is philosophically and theoretically underdeveloped? Philosophy and theory of EHE and other alternatives is a vital part of educational information. I suggest it is an area that needs development to mine the rich vein of knowledge it offers for *all* educational practices.

The emergence of EHE as a form of education that is gaining prominence and showing quantitative and qualitative success as education (see for example Rothermel, 2002; Rothermel, 2003; Thomas and Pattison, 2007) begins to show us new educational matters of pertinence to the mainstream, particularly where the mainstream aspires to the democratic underpinnings fit for citizenship (Crick, 1998; McLaughlin, 2000). The same is true for democratic educational alternatives: it is vitally important that these are better appreciated by mainstream educational studies (dominated by the 'ordinary' school) (Stronach, 2010).

Effective alternative paradigms within education as a field are possible. Within schooling *as* education as a field, they are not. Competition between and because of various forms of education develops practice and its outcomes, as well as healthy differences. Differing paradigms in this sense do not mean different kinds of schools: free schools, studio schools, academies, and so on. It means that each has a different theoretical base from another. Each paradigm is a different 'world' *because* of the fundamental differences underpinning its educational theory and pedagogy. Educational experience *as modality* differs. Thus, a free school set up along schooling lines is not outside of a schooling paradigm but within and a part of it, despite certain specific features of difference such as being set up by parents.

Given that paradigms are changeable with time and situation, it is interesting to note the resilience of the schooling paradigm within education (once we identify it as such), and how it continuously underpins the same general mentality of authoritarian and hierarchical structures. Certain commentators lament this resilience (see for example Harber, 2009b; Harber and Mncube, 2013). This inability to self-modify at deep structural levels of management is especially surprising given that such schooling as a modality bases itself on scientific principles of assessment, verification and reliability. If Kuhn is correct and science is a domain which, due to its need for precision, must continuously admit of anomalies and therefore in time a critical mass of these demanding a new paradigm (Kuhn, 1962), schooling should have changed paradigm by now. We might ask, what is wrong with schooling? Is an inability to evolve at deep levels of the 'self' of schooling an attractive quality? Is being unreflective of a clear mass of anomalies such as over-testing, teaching to the test, bullying, abuses of power, repression or disagreement with individual expression appropriate? Perhaps the answer is that education is still a very immature science and awaits its first paradigm shift, or perhaps it is not a science at all but has been masquerading as one to gain status, or perhaps Kuhn is wrong.

I suggest education *is* a kind of science that fits Kuhn's convincing model of paradigms and revolutionary shift, even if it is an 'elusive' and 'troubled' one (Condliffe Lagemann, 2002; Labaree, 2006). However, the idea of science presented by Kuhn may need to open its doors to new forms of 'science' that are paradigmatic and yet are not imbued with scientism. There is a challenge to 'linear' scientism here and the possible role of switching in our world. Instead of logical progression and developmental accumulation, social 'switching' may (and indeed seems to) occur through 'gateless gate' happenings; according to principles of reaction found in complex human nature. If switching occurs through gateless gates, an educational alternative is easier to recognise as an educational paradigm. But because scientism prevails we don't even need this ease for the situation to hold. Science says a switch shows a change that is possible. Needing 'order' is irrelevant.

Putting aside educationisms and opening oneself to the possibility that we do not know what education is or what it can achieve in the way of new forms of self flourishing, people could be re-turned and re-tuned to educational ideas refreshed and stimulated. We hardly know anything yet about education from a multi-paradigmatic *modality* perspective. In this regard R.S. Peters was right: 'there are many issues ... on which no work exists at all. What, for instance, is meant by "education"?' (Peters, 1973, p 3)

Notes

[1] Second generation home educators are those who were brought up with EHE as their educational mode during childhood. They have nothing to discover in the same way as first generation adults, although EHE might still be something 'sought' for such individuals, when they become adults and parents in a society used to schooling. My thanks to Dr Richard Davies, himself a home educator, for this distinction.

[2] A rich, extensive database of research on EHE is to be found here: www.icher.org.

FIVE

Moments of discovery

Street Survey Respondent 56: It's the first time I've thought about it ... There's a little light gone on in my head ... [*He smiles, winks at me appreciatively, takes the information sheet.*]

Introduction

So far there has been a lot of social and theoretical context setting. This was necessary to underpin on *other* terms of the educational what it is will now begin to be considered in the empirical data. The methodology for the interview extracts to follow can be found in the Appendix.

The moment of switch matters because it stands to restructure education. Crucial signs of gestalt switching will be shown in the latter part of this chapter. First, to recognise the fragility but power of the switch moment and its mirroring of a Kuhnian perspective on discovery and paradigm creation or unveiling, come *supporting* elements: aspects that allow and facilitate, as well as give meaning to, the discovery experience. These form a foundation for the realisation of difference that an educational alternative can bring. The data covers discovery of any alternative to mainstream provision, although EHE experiences dominate.

The interview testimonies are all about effects in the self and responses of the self; 'the self' meaning here, and throughout this book, the named individual with a unique identity. Following from discussion of Foucault's technology of the self these reactions and expressions seem like an interior rationale of the self answering and making sense to itself; people finding meaning (for themselves) in a new, elected world, full of surprise; involving active volition (and the joy of this), rather than blindly accepting the expected, given and assumed world.

Life-changing discovery

Discovery of EHE is an important life event for the people who have found it for the first time. With the various emotional, social, psychological, political impacts of EHE discovery, come a number of side effects shown in this data, often backed up elsewhere by other studies. Amongst them are: changed lifestyle (Arai, 1999; Neuman and Avriam, 2003); changed family relationships (Arai, 2000); changed perceptions of the politics of society, including a re-aligned attitude towards the formation of the democratic self (Meighan, 1984; Arai, 1999; Safran, 2008); changed ideas about community and changed perceptions of education and of pedagogical/heutagogical practice in the life of the child and also the adults in the family (Earl, 2006; Thomas and Pattison, 2007).

Joan discovered EHE as an Education BA undergraduate, during a lecture, when a film was shown about home education. As a result of this discovery she decided to pursue a particular life direction:

> **HL:** Did finding out about EHE change you in any way?
> **Joan:** Yer definitely, I think it has changed me. I think about things more ...
> **HL:** Has it transformed your self?
> **Joan:** ... It has transformed my self in that I would possibly consider home education for my children ... I probably wouldn't have thought of it before... my family are very conventional ... has it transformed my self? ...Yes, because if I hadn't read or accessed or had the lecture on home education or known about it so it wouldn't have got me on this path to know more about it [*doing postgraduate study on EHE*]. (April 2009)

Hannah spoke of how discovering that EHE was a possibility had a profound effect on her and required deep thought:

> **Hannah:** I talked and talked and talked to these people at the home ed group and they all said it isn't easy, not a bed of roses and think really hard about it and so I did think really hard. It was such a big step to take and it didn't seem like one you could go back on all that easily. So obviously you could send them back but once you'd started along that route, you're committing yourself to a whole new way of life and a whole new belief in the fact that school wasn't the be all and end all; there was another way to do it. So I thought it was a huge choice to make ... It was as big a change to reject that [*schooling*] as to reject the faith of your family. It feels that way to me. (July 2009)

Lynn discovered a new life when she discovered EHE and has been ever since a strong advocate of EHE practice and lifestyle:

> **Lynn:** I was forced into this [*due to unhappiness of son at school*] but it so quickly became a lifestyle choice and I see that over and over again – why would you want to go back to that when you could have this? ... although we're not anti-establishment over everything, we have stepped outside one box and see it for what it is: a box and we see other parts of it as other boxes, control boxes ...
>
> **HL:** So if a person is in a box that gives them a certain feeling and if they are outside of a box, what's that feeling?
>
> **Lynn:** Freedom to be what you want to be; choose to be what you want to be ... (July 2009)

Anna stated how EHE had changed her life:

> [*Following Lynn's comment to her about EHE being 'good for the soul':*]
>
> **Anna:** Where do I sign? [*Everyone present laughs.*] It has completely changed my approach to society and people and living and my children.
>
> **HL:** I assume for the better?
>
> **Anna:** Yes, well I think so definitely. Made me much more stroppy [*we laugh*]. But I think that's good. (July 2009)

Various of the interviewees found discovering EHE or thorough-going democratic education practice such as found in alternative schools, a liberating experience in terms of the life-changing properties it offered and the strong affect it had on them. This was both in terms of their personal outlook on life and their views on education:

> [*Speaking in context of going outside of classroom, as a teacher, to go bird watching with some boys:*]
>
> **Tom:** That opened my eyes ... seeing it is a different thing ... I'll tell you something that really opened my eyes ... [*I took*] these kids out bird watching ... these kids transformed ... they were just completely different as a result of this. Why? Because we had followed something they were interested in ... It really made an enormous difference to them ... their regular teacher said after a week 'My God! What have you done to them?' ... (March 2009)

HL: So what does matter?

Illona [*EHE mother*]: It's just simply being happy. Having a life you can just enjoy and look after yourself. I have a strong work ethic ...This seems to free us up. We feel much freer all of a sudden. That we could go, go abroad for a couple of years.

HL: Your children not being in school has had an effect on you as a human being?

Illona: Definitely! [*forthright*] I'm much more relaxed. [*Discussion re pointless homework assignments*] ... you start looking at education in a different light and you're saying well, what are they learning and it is all set down and in a box ... whereas we can learn whatever we like! That is an incredible freedom as well! (July 2009)

Sorena [*mother of a young daughter*]: ... it was just the idea of her going to school and being changed in any way and I had to learn to accept that, and I just thought there was something very, very wrong about having to be made to feel like that so, and when I realised that there was a choice and I didn't have to send her, then I suppose it just – just everything changed! I wasn't depressed or anything about it because probably I realised quite early on [*that you could choose to home educate*]. (July 2009)

Fred [*a newly trained supply teacher*]: To be honest I found because I was in the middle of this, umm no I wasn't, it was just before I started this placement at a school near [*names small town*] and I felt that my practice had been transformed by that one day [*at Sands School; a democratic school in Devon, UK, similar to Summerhill School in ethos*] that suddenly my relationship with the kids was totally different too and to any other school and I don't know how objective it's possible to be because it was a completely new school. I suppose if I'd been working in a school, had that experience, come back, and felt, oh this is totally different, um, because it seemed to me, I remember saying to the head teacher, you're clearly doing something right here because this is by far the best school I've taught in and then just thinking, actually the way I am being is different, and it was ... there was a sort of openness in me I think which partly being a supply teacher you can do because you know you've not got to get the results, so there's a bit more freedom to be who you are and teach in the way that you want, umm.

HL: You say that that experience at that school – just that one day – had transformed ...

Fred: hmmmm

HL: What is it that it had transformed?

Fred: [*long pause*] I think I just got a bit more honest with the children about my position on education and the reason we do it the way we do it, it's not because it's the way I believe it should be, but it's what we're required to do and ... but there's more an element of playing a game, errr, than me being a kind of figure, a sort of representative of this, um, system, which I don't ... erm, when I was trained as a teacher there was one thing I was taught was never to undermine the education system, you know you have to be a pawn of it and deliver it as though you really believe in it otherwise it'll just undermine everything and it'll all fall apart and I think after Sands [*school visit*], I kinda thought 'Naaah, bollocks to that,' ummm.

HL: You mean you don't ... like ...

Fred: err ... there's just a sense that we're doing this because this is what we have to do not because ... I just found myself in subtle ways saying yer I know this nonsense but we've got to do it. That's what we've been asked to do and then we'll get on with the fun stuff ... (May 2009)

HL: When did you find out it was possible to do that [*EHE*]?

EHE Family Mother: Well, I had a book called *Oxford for the Under Eights*. We didn't know anybody who was home educating at all but I knew I had to do something. [*Son*] couldn't stay there because his whole personality was changing – such an unhappy boy in school and so I knew I had to do something. So I was going through the book and I found a contact for *Education Otherwise* and phoned the lady. There was nothing that I said that she hadn't heard before and she told me what I could do and just then at that stage, because it's such an emotional time for anybody who's had a child who is unhappy in school – for whatever reasons it affects the whole family – and she said 'you can take your child out for a week, a month, two months, a term'. Because at the time you just think what do I do?

Um and so, that's what we did and deregistered from the school straight away.

HL: When you had that conversation with her how did it make you feel?

EHE Family Mother: Oh the relief! That I think I probably slept better that night than I had done for weeks, even though we had many sleepless nights afterwards because then the weight of the responsibility for the future ... it's only recently that I've thought well do I want all those advantages if they're not going to make me human? But the relief, ahhhh, it was tremendous. (July 2009)

Discovery of educational modalities different in nature and lifestyle context from those offered by mainstream schooling is not a whimsical matter. The depth of the issues which were revealed and relieved by discovery can be seen in the strong vocalisation of the relief felt at finding a solution.

> *[Discussed at HESFES home education summer festival:]*
> **Lynn:** I just feel that somebody took this weight ... I'm here still [*amongst home educators, despite her children being past school age*] because I cannot repay what this community gave to me. This community caught my family when we were falling. This lot saved the lives of my children. (July, 2009)

HL: Well, you're sort of painting a picture for me for how you must have felt getting this kind of treatment as a parent [*from the school*] and I'm wondering: how did you feel when you read the article [*about EHE*] in the newspaper?

Pippa [*mother of primary age boy*]: Umm, well that there was some sort of, I guess some sort of light at the end of the tunnel, that there was an alternative ... I suppose when I read the article I thought well, yes, homeschooling, that seems like a good idea, find out a bit more, because it gave us an alternative to what was going to happen long term for him ... you think, ok, there's something else to explore here, there is another possibility ... (March 2009)

HL: Can I take you back to that newspaper article? Did something happen to you when you read that newspaper article?

Pippa: Yes, the ten tonne weight sitting on my shoulder started to lift. I think, yes, when you can see other options, even if you don't know whether they are the right ones or not, even though you don't know whether they will work or if they're appropriate or whatever else, I think that seeing there are other ways which are legal and possible, yes ... and I think seeing that there were other ways, other possibilities, yes, just started to lift that weight. (March 2009)

Often, remembering the extent to which discovering EHE (in particular) offered release from difficulties and/or a new way forward, caused interviewees to well up into tears and briefly openly cry, until they (easily) regained their composure:

Sorena: ... I suppose it changed me in the sense that I just became freer. I just thought to myself, great! We don't have to do all those horrible things we can just continue as we're doing because we're just doing really well and we're all enjoying each other's company, why would we want to change that? This is brilliant and I just can't wait for every day. [*She starts to cry.*]

HL: You've just got emotional again didn't you? ... I mean, it's a happiness isn't it?

Sorena: Yeeeaah! [*Says smiling at me through her tears.*] (July, 2009)

[Speaking about an argument with a teacher who couldn't understand her son had a need for special equipment.]

Lynn: It was the last straw but it wasn't the only one and it was at that point that I just went on the internet again and somewhere I must have heard something about *Education Otherwise* ...

HL: Can I just ask you something [*inaudible – wind in recording equipment*] emotion because you looked like you were about to cry ...

Lynn: Yeah. My son wanted to kill himself. Yeah. So I must have seen something about *Education Otherwise*. I didn't know anything about home education, something, newspaper, television, something must have gone in and registered. (July 2009)

[Speaking in the context of experiences of problems with son's school:]
Pippa: ... but they were totally unrelenting in their 'this is their establishment they run it their way and if you don't like it tough basically' ... [*Talks about those who are outsiders or critical being unable to be fitted in: she cries.*] (March 2009)

Finding an alternative to their previous understanding of education has been personally impactful for these individuals. Their relief is connected to their love for their children and their child's personal and educational well-being. It is also relief for their own well-being, enhanced by EHE discovery, and that they can satisfy their status as parents with the responsibility they hold, in law, to ensure an education for their children. Instead of a difficult educational scenario, they have found one that works for them personally and thus for their familial responsibilities and family members, without being subject to the pressures of an enframing mentality. EHE and other alternative education discovery is being seen here as not only relief, but also careful and thoughtful volition – a wish to develop care for self and others – a joyful freedom becoming all too rare with an age of 'total parenting', (Smith, 2010) where 'a limited conception' prevails 'in which the place of caring is in danger of being lost' (Smedts, 2008, p 121).

Those who participate in home education often express the idea that there was an area in their life that was not satisfactory to them prior to discovery. As a consequence they were actively seeking or wishing that they could find solutions to a problem, which was found eventually in alternatives. The following comments are examples of this tendency:

[Tom, a teacher who became an academic of alternative education, was talking in the context of a new experience of being a member of the Labour Party and other ideas and activities when he was young.]
Tom: That was another eye opener, onto another world, so I was obviously looking for these and of course the more you do it, the more you look, so it kind of feeds on itself ... it was a part of all that looking for other things.
HL: It seems to me from the way you're talking about that period and your life in terms of finding out about these different worlds ... it seems that it was quite exciting.
Tom: Oh it was. Absolutely! Oh there's a new world ... I think I was trying to save my self really ... this is your sense of self coming out here because I'm facing all these contradictions ... I'm trying to reconcile all of these things and the only way I can reconcile all of these things and the only way I

can reconcile them is to come up with an alternative script [*banging table*] to all of this ... so I have to find another script for me and the only way you can find that is by searching for alternatives ... Certainly I was looking for an alternative script that could explain what I wanted to be and where I wanted to go and what was going on because I knew what I didn't like and I needed to find something I did. A new way forward ...

HL: What is this force in you?

Tom: I was uncomfortable. I wanted to restore the comfort, I wanted to find a way through that I could be comfortable with. I think all of us are looking for some form of balance in ourselves ... you got bored ... [*with the routine at university as a student*] ... actually you were looking for something else ... I want some meaning, something meaningful to me. (March 2009)

[Speaking in the context of day dreams of other lives:]

HL: Before that, did you have any dreams that were like that?

Elianne [*home educating mother*]: Gosh I don't know ... I still had an interesting life but I wanted something more ... it wasn't just about being in the mountains it was more about lifestyle I think.

HL: What is that 'more' thing?

Elianne: Well ... [*She asks for the recorder to be turned off. It is. We have a chat about why she wanted it switched off at that point. We turn it back on with her consent.*]

Elianne: Well, I think 'more' is something that is good ... [*talks about dreams*]

HL: What was it that appealed?

Elianne: I think to me what appealed was that they [*boys home educated in Montana, US, whom she had read about*] were able to achieve the same thing that they would supposedly have achieved if they'd been to school. They ended up going to Harvard and Yale and they achieved that without having to wear the uniform, line up, take the exams, get test answers wrong or right go through that whole deadly, dry process that I couldn't stand, you know, not that I didn't like my uniform but you know the whole sort of restriction the whole sort of, urrgh, tightness of being [*in*] school. (February 2009)

HL: So when did you start to get interested in alternative education?

Betty: ... I'm basically looking for something else! ... [*as a teacher in a mainstream school*]

HL: So when you heard me talking about home education was it a kind of 'oh what's home education?' moment?

Betty: Yes it was. I just wanted to find out more about it really ... I did go straight to Waterstone's after we met to look at the book you mentioned ... [*speaking about home educated children, whispering like it needs to be kept secret that she has said it*] They're just so lucky! (September 2009)

Research has already been conducted on the ways in which adopting EHE as an educational modality is a holistic change for families (Arai, 2000; Meighan, 1995; Neuman and Avriam, 2003; Rothermel, 2003). What we see here which is new, is the extent to which discovery is, in itself, an event. The nature of this event interacts with the self in ways that are transformative, emotional, liberating, serious and profound. Discovering EHE and alternative possibilities such as democratic approaches to schooling, opens up a significant and power-laden entrance of knowledge into a person's consciousness. This affects them at a personal level, with consequences in social, emotional, political and educational directions. Because any form of discovery will involve aspects of how they made the discovery, the following interview extracts present both details of sources of discovery as well as information about the effect of that discovery.

New ways to be and become

Discovery of alternative educational modalities of various kinds was being reported by interviewed participants as having served to open up possibilities of inner growth and development. This was similar in nature to aspects of self-development highlighted by Michel Foucault, discussed in Chapter Four. It came out in the data as a focus on seeing, changing and challenging visions of being. Embracing possibilities that new, hitherto unexplored ideas brought with them was exciting. A key feature of such explorations of new ways of being and becoming were remarks from participants about experiences of feeling a sense of well-being.

Nina [*German home educating mother*]: ... It's more like an equilibrium. I feel satisfied being in the right place doing the right thing. Most of the time. Not always but most of the time. Yep. Because when you are home educating you are more or less in control and whatever goes wrong it's your own fault. You can't blame it on anyone else but that gives you so much more choice ... (July 2009)

[Both Illona and Hannah talking about how they both wished they could have autonomous EHE-ed their children since the beginning:]
Hannah: School first and then picking up the pieces ...
Illona: I don't know if it's just that [*EHE friend*] is just an amazing person but her kids seem to soak up everything whereas the ones that are schooled first [*and are then home educated*] seem harder to involve in things I think ... one of her daughters ... I can't explain it any other way than that, but she knows who she is and she knows what she'll do and she knows what she doesn't do. She's not rude or naughty or anything like that. She's just assertive ... at five! Someone said it's because she hasn't been to school to have it all knocked out of her and I think that's possibly true.
HL: How do you as adults feel now [*that your children are educated out of school*]?
Hannah: ... mixed ... the main thing is a huge sense of responsibility that his [*son*] future is down to me to direct and if he doesn't achieve his potential it'll be my fault, if it's anyone's fault. And, the other it's just a great sense of enjoyment really, learning alongside him, which is just so nice, things I didn't bother with at school, I'm now going wooooh, along with him, going ooooah, and we go ooooah together! [*laughs*] It's really nice.
Illona: Yes, I think I'd say the same but the other way round. I'm not too bothered with it. I think he'll be fine. Whether other people think he'll be fine is something we'll have to cross when we come to it. (July 2009)

HL: Is EHE a change in life from before?
Lynn: It is a different life. The autonomous home educators tend to take on the whole thing ...
HL: How does it feel though?
Lynn: I have a happy life. I'm much less stressed. I have a lovely life! Happy people live in my house. I don't have much money ... we stopped chasing school and chasing

that and rush rush rush – we have time together as a family
... (July 2009)

Family Q Mother: I think for me ... I've been just amazed at
how they learn and just fascinated by watching that happen
... I don't know, it just all falls into place ...Why interrupt
that process? (September 2009)

All of these quotes are by people who were following, to various
degrees, autonomous home education. As we can see from these
comments such practice reduces feelings of stress and develops positivity.
This seems to be related to the absence of school measures, targets and
assessments as well as the daily grind of the schooling timetable (see
Thomas and Pattison, 2007; Bergeron, 2009). This grind can include
extracurricula commitments with various pressures to conform that
these might impose and which can lend itself to parents falling into
the westernised trap of over-parenting (Bernstein and Triger, 2010). In
EHE, needs can be met at a pace and in simple ways in tune with the
individual child and their parents, rather than as response to institutional
or social pressures. It is suggested that the discovery of EHE induces the
possibility for such ways of living peacefully. Of course, it is, as Illona
was told by other home educators, not all 'a bed of roses'. EHE can
be very hard work as well (Moore and Moore, 1988; Morton, 2010b).

The realisation of what EHE entails is part of the journey of discovery
and seems to involve a certain 'clearing of the eyes', to see with new
vision and the passage of time:

[About discovering the possibility of EHE when she was a teenager
– now home educating her children:]
Elianne: To me it seemed like yes, it's possible. People do
this out there. People are free to do that, erm, but for me I
didn't think it would ever happen. For me it seemed like a
big dream. I never thought it would be possible – I don't
know if I'm answering your question – liberation, yer, it
was a lovely liberating thought but I didn't think I'd be able
to apply it to myself.
HL: Why do you think that? Why did you think that?
Elianne: I guess when you've been, not indoctrinated, but
when you've been living a certain lifestyle, it becomes
quite embedded, doesn't it, that this is what we do, we
do our O-levels and then we do our A-Levels and then
we get our job, you know, and we follow the path that

everybody follows because this is the done thing and, um, you sometimes you don't think there's a way, because when you're thirteen and you're in boarding school, there's no sort of way out it seems anyway ... (February 2009)

Lynn: I'm just not that person. It's a steep learning curve ... B. [*husband*] and I have come on a much bigger path ... journey ... journey than the kids have, because we, we're indoctrinated in the other way for much longer. (July 2009)

Physically seeing or witnessing for oneself EHE ideas in operation provides assurance that, despite ingrained understandings, other *ways* are possible. Because these forms of education are so far removed from the vision that most people have of what education is and can be, actually seeing it happen with one's own eyes offers understanding. Again, the passage of time, in a sense of 'evolution' of concepts (see Toulmin, 1972) is sometimes – but not always – important:

[*When Joan was an undergraduate, her lecturer had shown a video of various home education scenarios:*]
Joan: I don't think I would have been so transformed if I hadn't watched the programme ... it made me reassess what the point of education was ... it transformed my viewpoint. (April 2009)

[*Sara had come into contact with alternative educational modalities and ideas through past discussion with the author and then taken up the knowledge and slowly applied it to her own family situation:*]
Sara: It's a jump into something that you ... it's not completely clear to most ... it's one of those experiences until you go through that, you don't really know what it's like. (July, 2010)

HL: I use that word 'converted'. Is it ... is it an appropriate word to use?
Lynn: Yeah because my sister is talking about home education positively to other people now and so is my mother, whereas before I don't ... it was something I did; her daughter did, but I don't think they ...
HL: Did you convert them to that more positive aspect, or your children, or just the way things worked out well or ...?
Lynn: I think it's just the way it's the end result. We have lots of people [*in the EHE community/network*] who don't have

supportive families and we're saying 'really sorry', you know, you can tell them all the information you have and you can put them in touch with other home educators and try to get them to see autonomous home education working if that's what we're talking about, erm, but it takes time. That is the only thing that will show – when they start seeing, trying to get them to see ... look at [*son*] how happy he is now and try and get them to reflect back from that to this or ... (July 2009)

Nina: ... then we [*she and her husband*] went to a parents' meeting for gifted children. We actually met a family who were doing it: as he [*husband*] put it 'They are doing it!' [*laughs*], very funny and we came to talk to them and they were very nice open and friendly and I think that was the point when he was convinced that it was doable because he had to meet somebody in real life ... (July 2009)

Elianne: Some random article I saw that I really liked and then a few years later I met a girl who was homeschooled – an American girl – my sister's friend and she was so lovely and so was her mum and I thought 'wow!' this is a real example of someone who does it and it just, it really, really, appealed to me. (February 2009)

So, to wish for change and then experientially understand that *change* is possible, is what EHE and other educational alternative modes currently represent in a world full of the idea of education as schooling. People are surprised that alternatives exist and that educational change is viable. To see, in the context of the discovery of alternatives, is to have realisations. Practical 'proof' seems to matter to people: something physical that gives a clear sign that another world operates in this one – the 'world of education as schooling'. The new, previously unknown world, now discovered as existing and valid within the 'old' world – the world which for some reason isn't functioning satisfactorily – matters a great deal on a personal level. It has meaning. What people are seeing in these situations seems to be shocking, amazing, astonishing and convincing to them. It provides a ticket or bridge over to another experience that they can personally have for themselves. This clear sense of surprise at discovery suggests discovery has happened suddenly rather than gradually, in a way similar to Kuhnian revolution, as discussed in Chapter Four.

The gestalt switch towards alternatives

The following interview extracts show revelations remembered. Each presents a sense of a gestalt switch and a shift of location of self occurring:

> **HL:** Was going bird watching with these boys ...?
>
> **Tom:** That made a huge difference to me. That's why I brought it up because it was at *that* moment ... it wasn't until I'd had this kind of concrete experience... that it really started to dawn on me that what we take for granted as 'must do' isn't 'must do' at all ....
>
> **HL:** So when you found that out, how did it feel?
>
> **Tom:** Well, it was revelationary! That was the beginning ... It sparked something in my head... none of these ... these are all sort of 'ptip' [*makes sound*] moments they kind of form a whole, the development of consciousness is quite a slow ...
>
> **HL:** You said 'ptip' moment, what do you mean?
>
> **Tom:** It's like a, you know, an eureka moment ... it was part of a jigsaw that fell into place. It was the first time that I thought ... 'I see, I see ...'
>
> **HL:** What did you see?
>
> **Tom:** What do you mean what did I see?
>
> **HL:** You said 'I see, I see.'
>
> **Tom:** I see that it doesn't have to be like this. There is an alternative way of doing this and probably a better way of doing things ... (March 2009)

> **HL:** ... have these 'moments of epiphany' as you call them been a surprise feature of home education or is it something that's connected to you as a person but wouldn't be in the lives of other home educators?
>
> **Nina:** No, I think they are connected to home education. Very much so. As I said we were basically doing home education anyway all the time and I just felt it's like a jigsaw some pieces just put together and then you've got this feeling everything fits. I think that's the feeling I have about it. (July 2009)

> **Pippa:** ... what you're trying to do is alleviate these things [*traumas felt deeply by the child in school*] as quickly as possible finding that there aren't possibilities or options and then

you suddenly read something and think 'There might be an option, there might be something else to do. Thank God for that, I feel a lot better now, I might have found a solution!' (March 2009)

HL: What do you think you did to them [*children in the school*] when you said 'I'm interested in your ideas'?

Bill [*a teacher with a democratic approach*]: I think it shocked them because it hadn't happened before.

HL: What sort of shock is that then?

Bill: It's the shock of the unexpected, isn't it? A teacher asking us what we think! That's a pretty big shock! (April 2009)

[I ask Nina about her story of attending the parents' evening and speaking with the home educators and ask what happened to them both as individual adults.]

HL: What happened there?

Nina: Um yer it's sort of this moment when it makes click ... we had read the books together I had read the books and gave it to him saying 'Hey, here, read this – it's very convincing, very interesting' and he did, but somehow it was all very theoretical, it was what some people did but not what we could do or what I could do, umm.

HL: What did you say about click?

Nina: ... I think it made click with him mainly because he saw that it was actually something we could do. It was possible. Before it was something in books ... yer, it was a moment when we met this couple because they said 'We are home educators' and it must have baffled him [*husband*] to meet somebody in person.

HL: How did he behave? You know him very well, so ...

Nina: Yer, he was quite excited. Before it was just reading the books and 'yer, sounds interesting' but then he was, it became more real, more realistic.

HL: Did he look happy?

Nina: Yer, I think so. Yer. It's difficult for husbands to be involved so much because most of the time he's not there but he could see that the children were not happy and that I was not happy and I think he was quite ... quite satisfied that we'd finally found something we could be happy with.

HL: Do you remember anything he said to you?

Nina: No, he mainly listened. It was so interesting listening to these people telling us about home education. We asked millions of questions in one hour ... (July 2009)

Sorena: You know my partner was a bit dubious at first and he was a bit, you know, it's a bit early, she's only two and maybe when she gets to school age you'll think twice, or we'll think twice about it. But after having this epiphany it just felt as though we maybe needed to look into it more, so we started looking into it, joined a home ed group locally, a very, very, small home ed group, erm ... (July 2009)

[I ask about the effect of EHE community on the life of Lynn herself.]
HL: But in a social sense I think I mean, not necessarily in a ... a ... a...
Lynn: Ahhh, there was a moment of epiphany, so it's changed completely, but I'd have lived that life and thought I'd have lived a worthwhile life before, but by God, this one's so much better!
HL: I see. (July 2009)

[Regarding son getting a B in GCSE English after having been predicted a D:]
Lynn: That's the moment I think my mother and sister finally believed ... I think they thought ... I don't know what they thought I was doing ... home education was a step too far ... and autonomous education ...
HL: What kind of belief is that?
Lynn: That it worked. (July 2009)

HL: What did you say again?
Sorena: I'm not sure but something about basically that home education and autonomous education are a little bit like religion ... yer it's like a religion or it's like religion in the sense that you believe in it regardless of what people, I mean, this is from my own personal experience. I think that a lot of people must come to it because they realise all of a sudden they have some sort of realisation, whatever that may be, that this is the right thing to do it's sort of, it is a little bit like enlightenment in that sense. (July 2009)

Nina: ... you've got this feeling everything fits. I think that's the feeling I have about it.

HL: What do you mean?

Nina: The peace. (July 2009)

Hannah: I likened it to changing your religion. I thought it was that big a change of life, it was like becoming a Catholic ... it just seemed that big a deal to me. (July 2009)

Sorena: ... so you have to go with your gut instinct ultimately, erm, and at the moment certainly my gut instinct and belief is this is the only way to do it and I would certainly consider moving and leaving the country if it meant I had to change ... sometimes I just think you know it's that strong, that people believe in this that, er, it is almost like a religion! In that sense yer ... outside of family I don't really go round preaching about home education partly because I don't have any proper experience about it yet it's just a belief in my head, erm, so, no I haven't really met anybody, certainly haven't discussed it. I know home educators who believe very strongly about what they're doing, urm, but I haven't discussed it in these terms with them I just don't feel there's any need I don't have to go around preaching about it, that's what I mean.

HL: When you say it's just like a religion, what for you is a religion?

Sorena: I suppose almost like having blind faith really that you believe something to be right and true regardless of the evidence that's there and I'm not a religious person per se you know I'm atheist, but I would, I suppose, the realisation that it was something that we could do as an option and the effect that it had on me I, would equate that to finding God or something like that because it was just so, erm, I don't know it was just so deep that, huuh [*she starts to cry*] ... I just feel so stupid [*hands me the recorder*] ... (July 2009)

Hannah: The way my husband and I thought about was, it was like being an alien on this planet, so we had to jump planets and go on a different planet [*laughs*] ... Sometimes it's just my husband and I and we just think we're the only people that think thoughts ... you know ... lots of different things and of course you do meet people who think the same and it doesn't feel such a different planet.

HL: What kind of thoughts would you find in your planet that wouldn't be on the other planet?

Hannah: That success isn't everything ... the normal goals ... there's only what's right for you ... see success in different ways ...

Illona: Yes, definitely. I think on the other planet the road to success is university and if you fall off that road then you're not successful and our road is very different to that ... a lot of people we know ... schooling their children to go to university, that to me doesn't really matter ...

HL: So what does matter?

Illona: It's just simply being happy. Having a life you can just enjoy and look after yourself. (July 2009)

Tom: You realise everything is interconnected (March 2009)

Following from the discovery of different ideas of education come different evaluations of self, society and other. Discovery of EHE acts as a highlighter of rights and responsibilities. Parents come to understand that they have educational options extending far beyond the idea of school attendance as a democratic or human right. They appreciate with full force the responsibility they have taken upon themselves for the education of their children. When they realise this combination of ideas, it opens gates to other ideas about their place in society and the ways in which they might function as citizens of that society. It also seems to begin development of an understanding of themselves as subject to 'educationism' – as an experience involving prejudice and bias, ignorance and hostility towards their self and lifestyle as educationally determined. When this occurs, for some it is the first time that they realise human rights are not a given but protected by law. Questions emerge over the extent to which EHE practice is a human right in the same manner that education as schooling is thus conceived. These questions link into other matters to do with the sovereignty of the person in a democracy. At a more personal level, the discovery of alternatives entails the discovery of another side to oneself, or other possibilities of self in the context of the wider community.

Nina: ... the problem was finding the right school so when we came over here we were looking for the right school. There were two we had in mind and we choose the better one, so we thought, but it wasn't a matter of finding the right school. It was a matter of finding the right way of educating and school, just any school, just couldn't be that right ... education – couldn't provide it. (July 2009)

HL: After someone has a religious experience or something like that they seem to change their life ... etc and they don't believe in the old life they had. Is this similar?

Lynn: I don't believe in that old life. That's why I can't go back to [*previous profession*] or I can't go back into that old life because I'm not that person and I couldn't 'bite' [*apply for*] that Sure Start job that I could easily do, because I don't believe in that system any more. So I can't perpetuate the system, erm, I'm sure there must be children that school does suit, but I just don't think it can be very many really. (July 2009)

[Speaking about work colleagues who didn't understand EHE as another kind of lifestyle:]

Lynn: ...They've no idea about considering the environment, erm, this idea of mutual respect between adults and children, the idea that I home educate, erm, let alone that I don't sit and teach maths and English workbooks and sit at the table ... You can see it blowing their minds and making them question all sorts of things. I won't let them spray all, all the chemical sprays by me, they've never given it a thought ... All sorts of things, I make them stop and consider ... have you considered the amount of energy that goes into a new car [*manufacture*] ... (July 2009)

Nina: ... there's a certain element of anarchy involved in it [*home education*] which probably there is, because it takes a certain frame of mind to go against the grain, to not actively, to not do what everybody else does. (July 2009)

Pippa: I suppose like most establishments they don't have the control over it... [*re failures of school provision*] so you think 'Ummm!, so why aren't they more encouraging of children that are learning in different ways?' But I think it's basically because they have very little control over it and if you have very little control over the way children are taught, and in the bigger sense allowed to grow and think, they then might have ideas that children in school don't [*think*] because it seems to me when you go into schools you're all taught to conform to think the same way, whereas I think that one of the major things about home education is trying to allow children to follow the way they think themselves ... (July 2009)

Samantha: ... people's reactions are interesting ... there's a little bit of a divide ...

HL: What do you mean by divide?

Samantha: I guess they think you're different, you're going to do it differently. You're not gonna be like everyone else.

HL: What makes you different?

Samantha: Not sending [*daughter*] to school. She's not going to go to school like all the people in her ... toddler group.

HL: Is it as simple as that?

Samantha: I think so. Perhaps. I dunno, 'praps a part of them thinks that's a good thing to do: 'I wish I could do that.' But perhaps they can't consider that concept; they're not willing to.

HL: If we imagine that this is possibly true is there anything that you could say well, perhaps it's because they're like this or like that?

Samantha: Umm, lots of people have said, 'Oh I'm surprised you want to be with her." Lots of people seem to want to get rid of their kids. They can't imagine, envisage wanting to spend 24 hours a day with them. They want to pack them off to school so they can have some time to themselves ... get on and do other things ... their attitude to parenting is quite different [*from mine*]. (September 2009)

Conclusion

Apart from the existence of Kuhnian realisation patterns of discovery (anomaly leads to discovery, leading to new worlds of perception and meaning) and Foucauldian care of the self behaviours and attitudes, is there an overarching theme from this data for educational understanding? I would sum this up as discovery of education without schools is *important*. This comes with implications. These are personal but also societal and political; even economic.

On the personal level, EHE offers relief from pain for parents and children, caused by problems with schooling. The focus with regards to unhappy school children is normally on those children, but this data shows the very real trauma that parents themselves can experience over school failure. That fall-out is too often missed in educational assessments of schooling problems. When it comes to parents there is, I suggest, an unrecognised injustice emerging from difficult schooling situations which also affect adults; whole families to the extent that it changes their lives. EHE discovery, in such cases, is both the sign of such deep effects and the solution.

Happily, awareness of an alternative solution offers something exciting and interesting, which can work well for a family dedicated to its practices. Societally it creates family units which are not following the herd: this brings diversity of lifestyles into being and into social networks. Politically, people empowered to think for themselves and act on those thoughts with conviction is the fulfilment of the democratic dream; an engaged citizenry. Home educators in particular are well known for their ability to speak up and advocate for their interests (Stevens, 2003a). Alternative thorough-going democratic educators also know how and when to take a stand (Summerhill School, 2000). Alternative educational scenarios foster critical thinking. Economically, a parent ceasing to work to home educate is an adult not in the workforce and not 'boosting' the economy from the workplace, but this is also a parent in the home paying loving attention to a child's development rather than perpetuating a latch-key culture: this will no doubt pay economic dividends for society in the long term because the home educated adult is someone who was likely well supported as a child and thus enabled to contribute to society.

Discovery of an educational alternative is at the heart of a great deal which is enlivening, despite the various difficulties it can bring in its wake, as discussed in this book. What matters is Freirian conscientisation, whereby awareness and conceptualisation of an issue are heightened (Freire, 1996) and do not 'remain distant' (p 36).

A surprising feature of the data was the language used to describe moments of discovery. It bore resemblance to language used in religious domains to describe religious conversion from non-believer to believer. This might indicate two things: (a) discovery of EHE is a very personal event at a deep level of the self, or (b) educational modal adherence could be a form of 'religious' belief (albeit it without being in the context of any known creed). As belief it would be similar to that indicated by John Dewey in *A common faith* (1960), where everyday life is discussed as having enough material for the mystical and spiritual but these are yet able to be understood through a secular lens.

The variety of *ways* in which discovery happened was significant: chance, self-determination or word of mouth, but rarely through deliberate supply of information. Home educators might play a conscious and deliberate role in 'spreading the word' through either enthusiasm or belief that other people ought to know about what they see as a good option. The means or methods by which discovery happens is determined by internet access, acquaintances, interactions with media reportage, personal research, and any possible way that knowledge can be communicated, but not particularly via state information. Discovery, at the level of information, is also something that happens through such informal avenues in sudden or gradual ways. Levels of cultural capital and their related conceptual frames for discovery may play a part. There is, the data suggests, currently no set pathway for discovery of EHE and other alternatives to schooling. This is why the theory of the 'gateless gate' of discovery – bringing no conclusive 'method' to discovery forward – and the irregular, personal pathway to it, is fitting.

Finally, as mentioned in previous chapters, a meta-finding that emerges from the data is the structure of knowledge that we currently have relating to the nature of education. That education is a paradigmatic field of study at the level of epistemology and ontology, concerns the nature of education itself, not just methodologies and their epistemology (Alexander, 2006). The idea of such a shift or turn as desirable and possibly in progress, as part of the curriculum of the future, is opened up in the Cambridge Primary Review research surveys by James Conroy and colleagues, wherein, interestingly, home education is identified as a 'paradigm' (Conroy et al, 2010).

By talking about shifts, clicks, enlightenment, realisations, 'ptip' moments and the like, home educators and practitioners of other alternatives to the mainstream are highlighting a paradigmatic terrain to education as a whole. This terrain is of all educational possibilities and structured so *we can change our mind* about education.

SIX

Against discovery of education without schools

Introduction

The previous two chapters laid out first a theoretical vision of why EHE is for individuals to discover and then empirical data about what happens when this discovery is made. Limitations imposed on and of this scene are now discussed. Understanding factors of marginality of EHE discovery can help appreciation of the social and political issues touched upon previously, as well as the educational aspects running throughout the book.

The UK government (as it relates to England) is well aware of the historical precedents within England of and for EHE as a legal and socially embedded practice. It is clear that attempting to prohibit EHE altogether would be met with significant opposition on grounds of civil liberties within the UK democracy and implications that would be too weighty for other areas of statute. The Badman Review was careful to clarify that the right to home educate would not be interfered with (Badman, 2009, p 8). Subsequent reports have strongly reiterated this (House of Commons Education Committee, 2012). Despite such 'support' for EHE, this support is not and has never been active, and perhaps *deliberately* so. In Chapter Three I highlighted how a change to this situation was asked for, with an attempt made by the Chair of the Education Select Committee to garner support within policy making, through the agreement of the Parliamentary Under-Secretary of State, Department for Education to become a 'champion' for EHE.

Government information about EHE: the status quo

The occasion of a request within government for an EHE champion to function there is part of an official scene of not 'championing' EHE at all. This is because any improvements at local authority level are left to authorities to get wrong or right on their own (see House of Commons Education Committee, 2013):

Q226 Chair: There is nothing uniform ever about opinions among home educators, so I should never suggest that, but a weight of opinion – certainly of those who came before us – from home educators was that they felt that the law and the 2007 guidance was sufficiently clear, and that there was not a need for clarification and new guidance. On the other hand, the three representatives we just had from local authorities suggested that there did need to be clarification and that some of their colleagues, who might have been less clear than they were as to the settlement, would be helped by that. Do you have any feeling as to whether the various bits of guidance – Children Missing Education, the 2007 guidance, various other bits – form a coherent whole or not?

Elizabeth Truss: I have not seen any evidence yet that there are significant reasons to change what we have at present, but I am, of course, open to hearing of arguments that that is not the case.

Chair: Fair enough.

Q227 Mr Ward: On the relationship with local authorities, are you, in the spirit of localism, comfortable with the fact that, according to the evidence we have received, 122 out of 152 authorities have content on their website either *ultra vires* or misleading in terms of what are legally the powers of local authorities?

Elizabeth Truss: Well, I am in favour of localism. If there is misleading information on the websites and the Department for Education is notified, we will follow up on that. I certainly do not think there should be misleading information, but there are different services provided by different local authorities, and it is up to the local electorate to hold those local authorities accountable for what they provide. Just as there is a danger with saying that home educators are responsible for educating their children and then introducing further regulations and legislation, there is also a danger with doing the same thing for local authorities. It is a challenge that Ministers in the Department for Education face: how that relationship is managed. You could make the same point over things like children's centres and how that takes place, but, as I say, I have not seen significant evidence that changing that balance and having more central control would have a beneficial effect.

(House of Commons Education Committee, 2012, p Ev 32)

There is a difficulty with a localism attitude for EHE. It does not address the conceptual deficit attached to EHE as educational practice mentioned previously in this book. It is true that local authorities get EHE information wrong. A large part of that is their lack of grasp of EHE as *educational difference* from schooling. This is an issue of ignorance about philosophy and theory and the practices of otherness these can underpin. Whilst local authority officials are not supposed to be educational philosophers, they are supposed to follow the law and too often this does not happen with regard to EHE (Rothermel, 2010).

Local authorities, following localism and as a consequence of ignorance of EHE perhaps, do not think that integrating and including EHE in information about *education* for parents is important. It is not seen as a parental 'right' to know about EHE as a part of the advice provided by local authorities on educational choice. EHE is not advertised or included in any active, positive, outreach way. Statutory guidance to local authorities merely suggests that providing information on home education is necessary for local authorities to fulfil their duties:

> The DCSF recommends that each local authority provides written information about elective home education that is clear, accurate and sets out the legal position, roles and responsibilities of both the local authority and parents. This information should be made available on local authority websites and in local community languages and alternative formats on request. (DCSF, 2007, p 5)

There is an assumption in this that providing information about EHE which is 'clear' and 'accurate' is easy. As we have seen, effectively and appropriately understanding EHE is not straightforward. It is complex. Understanding schooling is straightforward because most people have experience of it. Apart from the difficulties of concept, no guidance is provided about *how* EHE information should be (actively) shared with parents. A silence rests in that space. In a letter I sent, dated 25 May 2009, to Ed Balls, then Secretary of State for Children, Schools and Families, the following question was posed:

> Do you think that parents of children of school starting age are fully informed by the State of home based education as a viable and valid form of educational choice, that they could consider when deciding how to approach their child's education?

The reply, dated 19 June 2009, from an aide to Ed Balls, Claire Stephenson, states:

> We have made no assessment of the extent to which parents feel fully informed about their right to educate their children at home. In the guidelines for local authorities that we published in November 2007 about home education, we recommended that they provide written information and website links that inform parents about their right to home educate.

But there is no written information that *reaches out* to parents. They have to go and discover it. There is then a disparity between what is legally viable as an educational choice and what is known, because what is known needs to be discovered. This is not the case with mainstream schooling. The result is that discovery of EHE is entirely the responsibility of parents. The attitude on the part of the government towards EHE as an educational option seems currently to be that they do not *actively* endorse it, whatever the rhetoric about it being a viable option. Ironically, given how badly it is done, *theory* is the largest part of what EHE parents receive from the state in the way of support. This brings no limitation and is at no state cost. Following the report by the Education Committee cited in this book, the government response was significantly to continue to *not* offer financial or much other support to home educators (House of Commons Education Committee, 2013). Again, this serves to cap and keep capped numbers of home educators; as well as perpetuating the situation where access to this option is only available to more affluent families. The reality is that for the state, rhetoric alone makes more sense and leaving parents to largely fend for themselves is practical. What the situation clarifies – if clarification were needed – is that the current state version or vision of education is schooling. EHE is not state sanctioned but merely state tolerated. This is a limited educational vision.

Confusion and misinformation

The statutory guidelines for local authorities, published in 2007 by the then Department for Children, Schools and Families, offer advice about EHE assessments:

> Local authorities should recognise that there are many
> approaches to educational provision, not just a 'school at
> home' model. (DCSF, 2007, p 5)

Despite these clear guidelines – which will not be updated according to
the latest statement (House of Commons Education Committee, 2013)
– about the 'attitude' needed to be taken by the authorities towards
EHE, the situation in 2013 is still messy. The government's response
to the Education Committee's recommendation 5 on EHE support is
set out below the recommendation itself (in bold text):

> **Recommendation 5: We recommend that the
> Department for Education carry out an audit of
> local authorities' performance regarding home
> education, and the information they make available
> on their websites and elsewhere, and publish the
> results, ascertaining which local authorities are
> performing well with regard to home education. We
> consider that, far from damaging the Government's
> localism agenda, this review would fit well with the
> Department for Education's transparency drive.**
>
> We do not think it is for Government to audit local
> authorities on their performance on home education.
> (House of Commons Education Committee, 2013, p 2)

In other words, inaccurate information which has prevailed on 80% of
local authority websites, even since guidance was issued in 2007 stating
clearly that this should not be the case, is being allowed – on the same
terms as previously – to continue. The likelihood that information
about home education will improve across the 122 out of 152 local
authorities said to be displaying *ultra vires* information (House of
Commons Education Committee, 2012) is thus slim, based on past
record. There is no imperative placed on local authorities to fall into
any line of accuracy. They are entitled to get it wrong locally.

In 2013 the accolade for local authority who got it *most* wrong
went to South Gloucestershire (p Ev 74). But many others also get
it wrong, as Alison Sauer outlines in her evidence to the Education
Committee enquiry:

13. More and more authorities are demanding or implying:

- That parents must ask permission to home educate
- That parents must inform the LA
- Regular monitoring of the education by the LA is a duty
- Parents must satisfy the authority of the suitability of the education provided
- Home visits are compulsory
- They must see samples of work
- That the provision in a statement of educational special need is made by the parent (the parent is in law responsible for meeting the needs of the child, not making specified provision)

14. Not only is it the case that in law there is no right to demand the above but the Elective Home Education Guidelines [2007] specifically forbid LAs from making many of the above demands.

(House of Commons Education Committee, 2012, p Ev 74)

So there is an inaccurate attitude, leading to inaccurate information, leading to inappropriate behaviours on the part of local authorities, which in turn leads to difficult relationships with parents. It is the home educated children who suffer: from seeing their parents stressed, from not receiving proper LA support for their home education style (if wished for) and from not being able to access whatever LAs might have on offer, because, unsurprisingly, relationships between the home educators and the LAs are dysfunctional. Does every child matter? Even one being home educated?

There is a training issue here. The following excerpt describes a need for a more consistent grasp of EHE across the country *as education*, both directly and indirectly:

Q120 Craig Whittaker: So if it is open to interpretation, how do you train your officers? How do local authorities ensure a consistent approach? Because, without question, that does not appear to be the case.

Melissa Young: No. Well, I can only speak from our point of view, and as you know, we are part of a shared service with two other authorities, Knowsley and the Wirral, which we do to provide consistency. We are all qualified teachers who carry out this role. I personally have experience in both the primary and the secondary sections. So it is about listening to the parents and discussing with them what their aims are, what their philosophy is, and partly using common sense and the experience that I have, and then going from there.

Helen Sadler: In terms of training, I do not think that I know of any authority that offers training, as such, in home education, but I started in Leicestershire and somebody said, 'You need to get along to the Staffordshire Home Education Forum,' and I think I trained myself by going there.

(House of Commons Education Committee, 2012, p Ev 20)

The government's response to a recommendation, following from this conversation, that proper training ought to occur is 'that officers with responsibility for home education should be properly trained' (House of Commons Education Committee, 2013, p 2).

Assuming a trained teacher, acting as a home education officer, will understand EHE without specific EHE training is unfair on those officers. Teachers studying to teach in schools receive specific school-based training where they learn to understand *that* modality well. But with regards to EHE there is a need for relevant LA officers to receive professional job-specific training – and contact with home educators whom they can learn from – in what is another world of education from schooling: one different, unfamiliar and which makes demands of a different educational knowledge base and information set. This is so that the following observation from the enquiry into the Badman Review is not a continually repeated comment:

> Some of the parents present recounted difficult dealings with their local authority ... One family commented that most local authority officers who staff home education teams have come through the school system, have often worked in that system, and typically have no knowledge of home education. (Children, Schools and Families Committee, 2009, p 60)

And the issue is not just one for England. *Schoolhouse*, the Scottish EHE organisation, noted continuing awareness of this problem a year later:

> ... too many parents are still being routinely misinformed by their local authorities ... Local authorities are accountable to parents on behalf of their children, not the other way around.

It is therefore disappointing to note the ongoing reluctance of some public servants to provide parents with accurate information about the law relating to home education in Scotland, or even to direct them to the government's guidance which makes it clear where the responsibility for children's compulsory education lies. (Schoolhouse, 2010)

The blunders that local authorities cause in their dealings with EHE practitioners, who are (or become) experts in the difference it offers educationally, should be avoided. There is a general principle of 'fitness for purpose' that ought to apply in education because what happens educationally is extremely important: it is not good enough to have a haphazard approach. Doctors and lawyers are not allowed nor expected to 'roughly' get it right and so, too, applying a schooling mentality to EHE ought to be seen as unprofessional. Modalities matter in relation to advice and 'inspection' protocols.

Leave it alone

Another limitation on discovery of EHE is financial. There appears to be what amounts to a *deliberate* policy on the part of the government to ensure that EHE parents bear the financial burden of this educational choice. Despite most EHE parents being tax payers contributing to a national guaranteed unit of funding per school-aged pupil of circa £5,000 – the 2012/13 settlement without pupil premium (Jarrett and Bolton, 2012) – these parents see little, if any, of this money for their own school-aged child. The government's line, refuting the Education Committee's considered recommendations for examinations funding, is to state the following:

> The Government respects the right of parents to educate their children at home. It is possible for local authorities to provide financial support for home educators such as examination fees under section 19 of the Education Act 1996.
>
> However, home educating parents have always taken on the financial responsibility for the education of their children and the Government is not seeking to change this principle. (House of Commons Education Committee, 2013, p 4)

Thus discovery of EHE with a view to putting it into practice will be capped by the financial constraints on the parents. Parents on low incomes are less likely to be financially able to make EHE discovery an educational reality if they and their children are interested in pathways into successful adulthood that require examination excellence. This means that home education becomes, or remains, a predominantly elitist, private option as an element of the education 'system'. To say that this is a shame is an understatement. As much of the literature on home education in relation to school problems show, *leaving* the state educational system is sometimes a vital option for the well-being of a child and should not be reserved as an intact benefit for the wealthy. The school system in the UK is not sufficiently safe or robust in its ability to be beneficial and personalised, such that the positive alternative of EHE can be made unfeasible for those for whom it is a right fit.

EHE *work* as an educational and care of self contribution to society has fallen into the category of the private and the under-recognised, in the same way that housework and housewifery is a low status and unwaged labour in most parts of the world. That women are a large part of this 'workforce' explains, unfortunately, some of the politics treating the status of EHE as being ignorable in so many ways. The status of EHE educational work mirrors important debates about the 'unwaged' labour of housework and child rearing (see for example James and Dalla Costa, 1972; James, 2012). Is that women are often the main EHE educators a factor in not seeing any need to supply any financial assistance to home educators for a child's education?

The financial penalty is an additional responsibility for parents not mentioned in the legal statute of the Education Act. It is addressed, on the state's behalf, in the additional clarification of Article 2 of Protocol 1 of the European Convention on Human Rights, previously mentioned in Chapter Three, where the Convention states: 'No person shall be denied the right to education' so long as it is compatible '… with the avoidance of unreasonable public expenditure' (see Human Rights Act, 1998, Article Two of the First Protocol). In other words, the issue is whether home educators expecting some financial assistance to help them with their common legal responsibility for their child's home education is an 'unreasonable' expectation. Current policy suggests it is. Perhaps this will become open to realistic challenge in the future, if that is not possible now.

All in a muddle (again)?

Whilst there is certainly not radio silence about EHE in the UK (and specifically in England), there is a strange state of affairs. People are 'doing it for themselves' when it comes to discovering EHE. Those who opt for schooling provision are helped from early years through to school leaving age with carefully accurate information, most of which is available from the state. Information about home education is mostly inaccurate. It suffers from an *official* information deficit. Whereas, DIY information – mostly proliferating via the internet – is not part of state provision and is often excellent. When so much about education is captured and constrained by instrumental discourse (Conroy, 2004), there is a strange freedom about EHE.

Prior to the Badman period, information about EHE which was contributing to the discovery of EHE as a legal educational pathway, happened largely on the free market of media decisions about what made good journalism. Media stories fuel an increase in discovery due to the information they provide, but they also increase demands for further information. This is of a kind which could be argued falls within the remit of government due to its important educational *informative* nature. Yet, as mentioned, accurate information is rarely forthcoming from state involvement in EHE. The following Education Committee discussion highlights this *ir*responsibility:

> **Q135 Ian Mearns:** It seems to me that the pathways for the individual parent are many and varied in terms of how we are going to go about even investigating what they should be doing or should be thinking about doing in the future. I just cannot help but think that, for instance, the Department for Communities and Local Government has provided a very neat little pamphlet for people that live in, probably like the one I live in, a Tyneside flat in Gateshead. It is called The Party Wall etc Act 1996: explanatory booklet and is a guide to the Party Wall Act, so that I know my rights with regards to my neighbours and anything that we do in terms of the adjoining property. That is a Government-produced document. It is very easily accessible; it is very plain in terms of knowing what your rights are and where to go now for more information. Do you think the DfE should produce something like that about home education?
>
> **Helen Sadler:** I would like to be part of writing it.

Melissa Young: It is difficult. Yes, it would be helpful, again, if it was clear. I think home education is mentioned in numerous Government publications. It is mentioned in the Alternative Provision Census guidance – little bits here and there. One definitive piece of work would be useful.

Q136 Ian Mearns: One of the things that is clear to me is that home educators' experience of understanding their rights and understanding what they need to do in order to provide for their children adequately and properly, and then knowing what to do in terms of what support they can get from the local authority, varies massively, sometimes within authorities but also across the whole country, because of the differences between authorities and how different authorities treat the issue. Therefore, from my perspective, if somebody clever at Sanctuary Buildings were to pull all the strands together and put it all down in a few sheets of paper or into a booklet, at least it would be a starting point for people. (House of Commons Education Committee, 2012, p Ev 22)

This discussion goes on to highlight some of the interesting complexity of providing EHE information:

Melissa Young: The difficulty with writing that document is that, as you said, practice varies between local authorities, but also cohorts of families vary: an inner city cohort with hundreds of families differs very much from a rural community with, perhaps, home educators home educating because they have a limited access to schools in that area. So one document that fits all will be difficult.

Q137 Mr Ward: Good morning, first of all. On this definition of suitable education, is there not a danger that, as soon as you move towards a strict definition, you then start imposing your own sets of beliefs and values? ...

(House of Commons Education Committee, 2012, p Ev 22)

Information about and description of EHE with a view to coherent sharing and communication are troubling and troubled, because it is a moving target. As Thomas and Pattison say:

Home education can range from the highly structured, based on set curriculums and lessons, to the completely informal. Styles of education can change between children and over time, bringing a flexibility and dynamism that would be impossible in a formal setting. (Thomas and Pattison, 2010)

EHE evolves and this makes it what it is. It seems that a huge stumbling block for providing more information from the state lies in the issue of the definition of education. It might seem easy to achieve a definition, but it is in fact philosophically embedded in diverse debates. It is extremely complicated and difficult to do. The Badman Review commented itself on this matter: 'I believe it would be wrong to seek to legislate in pursuit of an all embracing definition of "suitable"' (Badman, 2009, p 8). It is an issue which is enmeshed with precedents, legality, international conventions and so much more. Simply changing it so it covers all parties who might opt for EHE with their own particular cultural, philosophical, religious framework is enough to create a silence. The conversation does not seem to evolve in any concrete or meaningful sense. For instance this discussion, three years after the Badman Review, covers the same ground:

> **Q118 Craig Whittaker:** Good morning. Melissa, you have just said that you feel as though the law is ambiguous.
> **Melissa Young:** Yes.
> **Q119 Craig Whittaker:** We have not found any evidence from home educators that it is. In fact, Alison Sauer said to us, 'I do think often [local authorities] do not understand the law ... I have done a survey of all the local authority websites and there are only 30 that do not have *ultra vires* requirements on their websites – 30 out of 152'. Where is the ambiguity?
> **Melissa Young:** From our point of view, it is the fact that it is open to interpretation. There is no definition of what is suitable education. There is no definition of what is efficient. So because home education varies so much in educational philosophy and parents are doing it for so many different reasons, it is open to interpretation on the part of the local authority as to whether that meets statutory requirements.

Followed shortly after by:

> **Q128 Chair:** Specifically on the guidance, because we have the Children Missing Education guidance 2009, you have

the Elective Home Education guidance 2007. You have the different laws sitting in the background on that. Do we need new guidance issued from Government or do we just need greater clarity and understanding of the current situation as it stands?

Melissa Young: I would be happy with greater clarity.

Helen Sadler: Yes, I would.

Melissa Young: If there was a definition of what is suitable. I know through case law that the statement I cling to through all my home visits is, 'Will the education limit future life chances?' That is how I judge suitable, personally, and that is looking at cases that have gone through court over recent years.

Q129 Chair: Mind you, it is hard to imagine any form of education that in some way did not limit your life chances. Whatever form you take, it is going to exclude some things, or emphasise one over another. Is that practically applicable?

Melissa Young: Yes. A third of my cohort is Traveller children. If they have illiterate parents and that leads to a child not being able to read or write, then I would interrupt that [*EHE practice*] as limiting their future life chances whatever they do in their later life. It is applying common sense to this as well.

Q130 Chair: But you are saying that, none the less, you would like a new definition, and if it is not in case law, it would probably have to be in statute, and that would doubtless come with guidance to go with it. I do not want to put words in your mouth about that, which I probably just have.

Melissa Young: Guidance, as long as it was clear and there was, as I say, no ambiguity on either side – parents or LA or any other service involved with home educating families.

Q131 Chair: I am not a lawyer either, but I think if we were to have a new legal definition that was going to be applicable in the courts, then it would need to be passed in legislation. Do you think it is sufficiently important to have primary legislation that gives a definition of what suitable education means?

Melissa Young: Yes.

Q132 Chair: Elaine, your thoughts.

Elaine Grant: Yes, I think it is.

> **Q133 Chair:** So you would like a new statutory definition
> of what suitable education is. You are not happy with the
> case law definition.
> **Elaine Grant:** I think it is just too open to interpretation.
> **Q134 Chair:** Right. And Helen?
> **Helen Sadler:** I agree.
> (House of Commons Education Committee, 2012, p Ev 22)

This continuing lack of definition raises serious questions about the
relationship of the state to educational modalities of difference from
mainstream educational practice. It raises issues of significance with
regard to what we understand education to be and to be for. Yet,
aiming for a tidy outcome for EHE local authority inspectors and state
provision about information to do with EHE will always be unrealistic.
It should be a problem. A definition beyond the extent currently in
place is a catastrophic proposition. Because of the broad nature of
education (not specifically the nature of home education), being able
to define education is an approach closer to a 'soft totalitarianism' (see
Smith, 2010, p 358) than a democratic one. Why? Because determining
education determines (excludes also) who we are and can be. In so
many domains and ways, this is just plain wrong (see for example Facer,
2012). Education as a concept must be open to multiplicity.

However, what we can hope for at the very least is *accurate information*
from the state about what *can* be currently said to be the case, surely?

EHE information for discovery: a public service?

As we have seen, the state is not taking *active* responsibility for helping
parents who are interested in understanding EHE as alternative
educational provision. The following is just one example from the
study supporting this book, where concern is voiced along these
lines. The research participant is talking about the moment she
discovered that EHE was legal and viable:

> **Katrina:** I felt empowered I suppose, you know, actually I can
> do something about it and there is an alternative and I read
> everything I could find ... and I thought yes we have got
> rights as parents and I thought yer ... you know ... I wish
> I'd been aware of that right from the beginning.
> **HL:** Why?
> **Katrina:** Because I think, because I feel my children weren't
> happy ...

HL: As a parent, what do you do? [*re EHE*]

Katrina: You can't unless you know about it beforehand, because nobody informs you of these things. You don't go into the education system, they say well actually you can teach your child at home: did you know that? So unless you hear from other parents who home educate, it is actually very difficult to realise you can do it, that it's an option.

HL: Do you think they should be told?

Katrina: ...perhaps they should ...I think there's some danger in parents taking their children out for other reasons ... [*Gives example of woman who took children out and is doing autonomous EHE. Katrina then goes on to express jealousy and admiration for this mother's 'bravery' to do things differently.*] (March 2009)

Because of the rise of discovery – or at least a steady development in numbers through discovery – UK EHE charities suggest that they are acting as some kind of in-depth educational and sometimes even personal counselling service. A comment by a leading English charity member concerned with EHE, highlights the matter:

Sophia: Some people now haven't got the same 70s idea. They are just: 'Tell me where the action is!' like someone else will do it. There's a culture clash sometimes. They might have a lot of baggage about how badly things went at school ...We say to them: 'When you see the person from the council it might be strategically best to not go on for ages about how you were badly treated by the school ...'. (May 2010)

The lack of any action on the part of the state regarding communicating the possibility of EHE as an educational option raises questions and issues. Amongst these is: do tax payers have a right to be made aware by the state of various choices regarding educational *modality*, location and philosophy for their children? Could this perhaps follow a model where NHS patients are offered a *choice* of hospitals when they need to book an appointment? For this latter choice a state funded system is in place but educational choice is limited in ways yet to be conscientised. Should the state do something about this lack of modality diversity, given it currently still carries a significant educational remit? Parents, as data in this book suggests, want to know more and about different options.

National truancy levels are at an all time high with a government report in March 2010 of a 44% increase since Labour came to power in 1997 (DCSF, 2010). Not only that, but 'the number of parents prosecuted over their children's truancy has soared to 9,506 in 2008 from 1,961 in 2001' (Shepherd, 2010b). Bullying levels in schools are also far from minor, with over half (54%) of children in a DfES and Childline survey saying they thought bullying in schools was an issue, adding also that it was a 'big problem' (Oliver and Kandappa, 2003). Given such challenges, ought EHE to be given as *a positive option* that is available through government funded broad(er) educational provision and if not, why not? Is it wrong to discover EHE?

Evidence by local authority officials was given during the Education Committee's enquiry into the 2009 Badman Review, condemning as irresponsible headteachers who suggest to parents of children facing exclusion or similar difficulties that EHE is an option (Children, Schools and Families Committee, 2009). In the 2012 Education Committee enquiry on EHE support, this issue came up again:

> **Elaine Grant:** I think it is useful. I try to work with schools to allow a cooling off period. I do not like the phrase 'cooling off'. I tend to say to the school, 'Can you give me time to meet with the family and establish exactly what the story is?' because I only hear one side of it from the school. It is different when the parent comes and the child is being bullied and the school has written them a letter and said to the parent, 'Sign it,' and the parent turns up at my office and I say, 'So you are home educating?' 'Yes, when are you sending the tutor round?' 'We are not sending a tutor round. You have taken responsibility,' and they are horrified. They are absolutely horrified that they have taken that on.
>
> **Q166 Chair:** So you have had examples in your area where schools have sent a letter to the parents in order to get that child removed from their roll.
>
> **Elaine Grant:** Yes. So the cooling off period is useful to challenge school practice.
>
> (House of Commons Education Committee, 2012, p Ev 25)

Obviously it is not ideal for parents to be taking on EHE only when it is mentioned by their child's school as relevant to problems, and without having genuinely and sincerely 'discovered' it as an option. However, is school staff discussing with parents the idea of EHE *as an option* really so terrible? School staff are educationists. Why should an educationist not talk about education? The silencing of teachers who might value the option of EHE is something I personally experienced as a local authority educational provision co-ordinator for children out of school due to ill health. I was told that I could not and should not mention EHE as an option, as I would be seen to be not doing my job. Yet for some of the children and parents I encountered it could have been a positive and viable pathway. I also had a fairly good understanding of EHE so I could have been responsible and accurate in my imparting of information about it. Training in this regard would also then be necessary for headteachers, not just LA officials.

Participants in the street survey cited in Chapter Two showed both sides of the opinion divide: some thought that some parents of some children should not be told about EHE. Others expressed a desire for headteachers to offer information about EHE as an option in cases where there are difficulties with school. One woman said "it could be a recommendation" (Respondent 32). She had no problem with the idea that an educational professional would share knowledge of the various educational options available to her child and to her as a parent with responsibility in law for the child's education.

So why does the government maintain a stance which is negative towards the provision of information about EHE discovery as a genuine educational option forward, when school-based problems occur? Is this 'educationism' bias and prejudice, a strategy, common sense, ignorance, or a lack of understanding of education as broad and diverse?

Conclusion

As we can see, contexts for the discovery of EHE are politically, socially, legally and personally complex and wide-ranging. Moreover perceptions of EHE play a large part in determining both discovery and the information that might lead to discovery. Ascertaining a clear course through the various contexts is no easy task. Understanding what is right and wrong about discovery is difficult. This book sets up a context for 'genuine' discovery within positive family scenarios, which Chapter Eight addresses as a framework for understanding, along with less satisfying scenarios of discovery. Discovery of EHE by families blessed with positive features is still a challenge for those families, because discovery remains a socially and politically problematised act (if no longer legally so). This occurs in ways manifesting as unnecessary forms of interference or ignorance. The difficulties inherent in discovering EHE are not inherent to EHE practice itself. They are a construct from schooling as dominant that obstructs EHE practice.

Official understanding of EHE needs improvement. In order to achieve that appropriately, more respect for those whose personal and professional lives involve significant contact with EHE is required, including greater respect for research on EHE (see Badman, 2009, p 36). A fresh look at education as a state provision, to mean not *just* schooling, is open to national active debate and challenge. Such debate is long overdue and rings true with Michael Gove's April 2013 comment during a conference that 'we can't afford to have an education system that was essentially set in the 19th century' (Adams and Shepherd, 2013).

Much can be done – if the willingness is there – to recast education as a parental responsibility and a state function that is modal in nature: involving both mainstream schooling and educational alternative practice options. Yet the intractable differences of modality between schooling and EHE pose problems that are far too significant to be solved by a line of guidance from government. Discovery of EHE is a deep and tangled event.

SEVEN

School exit and home education

Introduction

There are viable alternatives to attending mainstream schooling which will allow education to happen. Some people are interested in these alternative options. They search for them. They need to *discover* them. But why would anyone bother?

This chapter looks at exit from schooling attendance as a phenomenon involving children intentionally deregistered from school rolls, but who once attended. It considers some of the reasons why leaving a school for home education might be a sane and important move. There are many factors that contribute to school exit. They interact and overlap to result in a deregistration. In the data in Chapter Five, some of the parents quoted there talked about difficulties they had had with their child's schools, resulting in a stand-off and lack of resolution. EHE was the resolution found. In connection to this I mentioned the harm articulated that was being done to such parents *by schools*.

What this chapter focuses on is why responding to such harms – for both children and parents – is part of a wider picture where schooling fails people. A theory is used here of 'exit'. This helps us understand better the reasons for movement towards EHE that discovery causes and follows. It also clarifies the nature of the 'gate' to escape from the school which is opened by discovery.

What is school exit?

The term 'school exit' is not new. In various research documents in the US, usage refers to school leaving age or school drop-out (Lloyd and Mensch, 2006; Papay et al, 2008). Here 'school exit' signifies another phenomenon, perhaps new in its scope and in its accepted legality as exit. There has always been truancy and absenteeism in the context of compulsory *seeming* (see Lees, 2013b) schooling. Now there is a substantial level of exit of a different kind. Facilitated by a rise in global awareness – *or discovery* – of the legal possibility of education through a modality of educational practice that is an alternative to mainstream school attendance, parents and their children exit schools for another pathway; in particular towards EHE.

'School exit' is a deliberate turning away, or a desperate running away, from mainstream schooling as a source of educational development. It is in this sense possible to include in it the idea of truancy or even school refusal and phobia. However, these are complicated issues intricately bound to schools and involving also matters beyond the educational. So, here it is divorced from such misalliances. 'School exit' involves elements of *choice* by parents and children to remove themselves from the pedagogic, social and material technology of mainstream schooling (and usually schools as institutions also) as a way to become educated.

This idea of freedom must take into account that much school exit into EHE starts as a reaction to a schooling problem, leaving no other choice than to get out. Families are pushed out of the school system through the necessity of protecting their children from harm or for the sake of attaining adequate educational provision, etcetera (see for example Parsons and Lewis, 2010). But I also want to point to the *act* of exit and highlight it; not just point at troubling causes. There is an exit which is chosen exit. This is when it becomes a decision taken within the scope of various options, of which one might be staying in or attending a school. Exit is a deliberate, careful and uncoerced act of turning the back on schooling as full-time attendance. In such a scenario, parents exit a hegemonic assumption of school attendance (for their children) and vote with their feet for the minority alternative.

Based on concepts of behaviour that Albert O. Hirschman proposed, a theory can be constructed which fits very well onto a schooling paradigm. It needs to be seen from a perspective of choice, facilitated by knowledge that schooling is not compulsory. In the UK and elsewhere where English is the native language this legally applies, but not in all countries.

In Hirschman's theory, consumers are (theoretically) free to see exit as a choice in these domains. People don't buy the product, or they move to other retailers, or change tastes. With regard to membership of the workplace Hirschman's theory suggests that individuals in institutional settings need a voice. Either they receive some measure of space and facility in their communal arena to *voice* their opinions about how things are done, or they will exit if there is an actual or perceived deterioration in practice. In effect their personal choices are stark: to voice their concerns to be heard or exit the institution if not heard (Hirschman, 1970).

'Exit' is associated with self-selecting action and the free market, whereas 'voice' is associated with political discussion of some form, with a view to improving conditions and working experience. Loyalty plays a part in this dynamic, for if there is loyalty to a firm, country or organisation (and its paradigm of practice) then voice is more likely to be opted for and tried for as a solution to difficulties. This helps employees to feel that they are valued for their voice and its contribution. But sometimes this can be blocked. People can receive messages that they are institutionally 'off message' and are then silenced (Fine, 1987; Zerubavel, 2006). In such cases exit need not be a literal movement of the body away and out; it can also or alternatively be mental and emotional.

In a school-based scenario, exit, voice and loyalty play themselves out. Exit of the mind and affections might be seen in the disaffection from learning participation amongst some school students (Marsh et al, 1978; Willis, 1981; Harber, 2008). Also, by losing the young people's interest and then possibly developing punitive strategies to bring them back 'on task', alienating them from affection, loyalty is lost; adherence falters.

In countries where alternatives to mainstream schooling, such as EHE, are legal, exit not just of the mind and affections but also of the body is permissible. A child does not have to go to school. They can exit the whole idea. Their 'educational movement' is unconstrained. But this is not true for schooling scenarios in some countries where school attendance is compulsory. People locked into compulsory schooling laws (for example, in Germany) cannot exit – they can only (attempt) voice (Spiegler, 2003).

There has always been substantial mental and emotional 'exit' *within* schools that struggled for resolutions (or age-related release) with and from schools. But, the scene is changing. Now, the number of people discovering and opting for home education around the world shows that the school gates are often open, not closed. Children can literally walk out. Indeed if 'exit' from the idea of schooling occurred prior to registration with a school, they need never walk through the school gates in their lifetime. I appreciate that there are fierce criticisms of this facility. Michael Apple is one such critic; seeing the option for exit as a detriment to democratic society-building through common schooling (Apple, 2000a). Whilst these matters are complicated and they deserve extended debate to deal with issues around exit, such as children being enabled through their education to change community if wished for and needed in later life (see for example McAvoy, 2012), the dynamics for and against are not here my concern. I point to the fact and possibility of exit. Furthermore it is suggested that the simple fact and possibility of school exit is a good thing for *education*. Dealing with the more complex aspects of education and exit facility in and for societies and their politics is another book. I can only bring limited elements of such debates into this discussion of the impact of a new structure for education through EHE possibility and its discovery.

Much of school exit into EHE as the preferred option is a co-created scenario whereby the organisation of the school must take its part in a responsibility towards failures to thrive and a lack of voice to resolve problems – resulting in dissatisfaction and exit. Such a stance of holding schools to account has, naturally, already been mooted in research literature (Pilkington and Piersel, 1991; Carlen et al, 1992; Yoneyama, 1999; Harber, 2004; Fortune-Wood, 2007; Harber, 2008; Harber, 2009b; Lees and Peim, 2013; Peim, 2013). These debates might be an axis point for deep developments with regard to education as a whole.

One example of such developments, of relevance to alternative pathways, could be a reinterpretation of truancy, school refusal or even school-based disaffection – as forms of Hirschmanian exit (Hirschman, 1970) from schools and school attendance. Exit being either of the mind and/or body. If schools can be seen to be at least partly at fault for exit behaviours, the *whole* onus is taken off truants, refusers and the disaffected. A more just and balanced approach prevails with just emphasis on elements of voice (Carlen et al, 1992).

If reasons for 'bad' behaviour are found to be not necessarily the fault of the malefactors, the matter is able to be looked at with advocates on both sides being equally empowered to say that what occurs is wrong. A child may have behaved badly one morning but who, what, how, where and when were the rules for bad behaviour agreed? Justification may currently rest with the rules of a school, but a perspective fundamentally challenging those rules and their reasons can advocate for the child having a reason and being reasonable in disagreeing with the rules. This is common discussion practice in democratically enabled schools through Meeting forums (Fielding, 2013). It is not common as an attitude in many mainstream schools and challenges to rules are seen too often as blanket insubordination because there is no forum where disagreement can be expressed. Yet, 'insubordination' might have a great deal of sense about it (Marsh et al, 1978; Henry, 2013).

Talking things through in a community is a theme in line with various ways of thinking exemplified in the alternative educational movement (for example Lane, 1928; Curry, 1947; Wills, 1947; Neill, 1968; Fielding and Moss, 2011). These offer perspectives whereby what is wrong with schools can be actually addressed at its deepest levels. From an *other* view than current hierarchical and authoritarian schooling's perspective, it is an abnegation of educational responsibility if mainstream schooling does not take the *voice* of the disaffected and badly behaved, or just plain different, very seriously.

School exit, following Hirschman's theory, is walking out because you haven't been heard and you stop caring. This is a tragic loss of affection. Schooling that does not listen looses. Leavers look for another, other, better vision.

Why exit?

One of the main problems that some critics identify with mainstream schooling is a (fixable) democratic deficit (Fielding and Moss, 2011). Whereas the purpose of schooling for all is linked to creation of democratically minded citizens in many countries, reality does not match this promise. Empirical research considering specific education *for* democracy programmes highlights this wide-ranging deficiency (Harber and Mncube, 2013). Instead what occurs is a disjunction between what schools say they do educationally for democratic outcomes and the authoritarian way they do it. This leads to agendas such as citizenship lessons falling short of success (Harber, 2009a) and schooling being, after all, an inevitably undemocratic experience that encloses, enframes and determines (Flint and Peim, 2012).

Another issue is that schools hurt people; physically, mentally and emotionally, and too few listen or act. Problems range internationally. Abuses of a sexual and violent nature as part of a dynamic of coercion on the part of teachers, have been documented in some developing world schools (Harber, 2004). In American schools black parents increasingly choose to pull their children from school into EHE because 'There were lots of fights and people getting shot' (Wheeler, 2012). Schooling for some can be toxic (Harber, 2009b). It can deny, silence, ignore, exclude, mislead, inculcate, fail and fail to protect (Bowles and Gintis, 1976; Marsh et al, 1978; Willis, 1981; McCulloch, 1998; Leander, 2002; Osler, 2006; Tobin and Ybarra, 2008). Bullying is a common schooling problem, affecting particularly those who are homosexual, disabled, poor or different, such as those from a gypsy culture (Campbell, 2005; Walton, 2005; Bloom, 2009; Maddern, 2009). There are also more tacit abuses to consider. This is where an individual sense of self is stigmatised or denigrated (Olson, 2009). Given the systematic nature of schools to educate towards and for certain kinds of outcomes and people, denigrating, failing and excluding some is perhaps inevitable (McCulloch, 1998).

With such a background of possible harms from schooling attendance, is it any wonder many people refuse to go if they come into contact with this at a personal level? They opt out in various ways: through truancy, school refusal and phobia and many even get 'creative', exhibiting extreme but effective hermit-like behaviours, for instance (Carlen et al, 1992; Yoneyama, 2000; Fortune-Wood, 2007). Sometimes getting out is a way to save one's life. Children can feel suicidal when faced with what seems to them to be intractable problems in their school environment. Sadly, some children do harm or even kill themselves on account of schooling experiences (Marr and Field, 2001; Staff Writer, 2008). Stories told by parents who have pulled their children out of schooling and into home education because of such feelings are common. Accounts of reasons why children feel unsafe to attend schools and the subsequent self-harm they wish for or attempt are often shocking. For instance:

> Mother: ... And you [aged 11] got taped up on the bus, didn't you by the older boys [aged 15]?
> Son: Yeah, and the driver didn't do a thing, which is kind of irresponsible, isn't it? ... Taped my mouth and then taped my hands behind my back and my feet and that. (Wray and Thomas, 2013, p 69)

or:

> 'Physically he (subconsciously) suppressed going to the toilet to the extent that he could go for a week without moving his bowels. Obviously when he did eventually go at home it was really painful, usually included some bleeding and took ages.' (p 72)

or:

> Mother: ... [he said] "I would like to knife myself. I'm going to go and get a knife and stick it in my stomach" and I mean this was an eight-year-old ... (p 71)

The stories portray school systems without power to keep children physically or psychologically safe to, from and in school: danger that occurs on account of school attendance.

The 'light at the end of the tunnel' of EHE discovery, which the interviewee Pippa talked about in Chapter Five, offers escape. It is a way to be free from entanglement in the less positive aspects of school as an institutional. Wray and Thomas's research article, from which the above excerpts come, goes on to show in further EHE practitioner post-schooling testimonies that for children traumatised by school violence, home education can resolve the emotional pain of violent schooling experiences (Wray and Thomas, 2013). People who home educate and who are home educated talk animatedly and with deep sincerity about the joy and pleasure they get from their new educational experiences. They commonly report feeling empowered, stimulated, encouraged, free and happy (Lees, 2011a). They claim that EHE offers them 'a sense of self,' in ways schools never did (Sheffer, 1995). School exit was a good choice.

In the face of some of the issues above of various violences and lack of voice and subsequent resolutions on account of EHE practice, ought there to be a *right* for parents and children to experience this educational option if they wish? This idea would be part of the general sense of the ethos for human rights construction: that what is beneficial to human life ought to be protected for them to experience.

A human right to *discover* EHE (and alternatives to mainstream schooling)?

In Chapter Six, Katrina talked about being sorry she hadn't discovered EHE in a timely and proper way. She said: "... and I thought, yes, we have got rights as parents and I thought yer ... you know ... I wish I'd been aware of that right from the beginning". What Katrina doesn't know perhaps, but is asking wistfully for, is that a 'right' *to know about EHE* as education doesn't exist. This is why *discovering* it is so important.

It is not possible here to get into the vast literature and complex arguments around human rights. What I simply highlight now is that there is nothing to protect a possible right to be aware of education that is in the form of EHE (and thorough-going democratic schooling models). Essentially there are many questions to engage with, such as: Should parents need to rely on discovery? Should knowledge about EHE as an option be a fundamental part of the human rights relating to education that we have? Should there be a 'differentiated right' – for want of better phrasing – one that involves the idea that education is modal and parents have human rights to education *broadly* conceived? Should differentiated rights be *explicitly* included in those rights regarding education, with an explanation of what that means? If not and because of such a lack, does otherwise the human right to education and the child's right to it, revert always to the school option?

The following example of the tensions involved in such questions illustrates the point: The United Nations Declaration of Human

Rights, Article 26(3), previously mentioned, clearly states that 'Parents have a prior right to choose the kind of education that shall be given to their children' (United Nations, 1948). Yet, other aspects of the declaration such as Article 26(2): 'Education shall be directed to the full development of the human personality and to the strengthening of respect for human rights and fundamental freedoms ...' mean that interpretation of the discovery of EHE is subject to different pressures.

One English example would be the situation where a parent who freely decides and chooses to avoid truancy fines and court appearances because of the non-attendance of their child at school, deregisters their child under the law that covers EHE and thereby avoids prosecution of any kind (at least for a while). This is what I call in Chapter Eight 'excuse' discovery: it is not a fully free choice and some kind of schooling may actually be a preferred option for these parents. Yet, whilst such discovery perhaps starts as an 'excuse', it might emerge as fruitful and positive given time as with other examples of *growing into* EHE (Safran, 2010). It might become an option 'directed to the full development of the human personality and to the strengthening of respect for human rights and fundamental freedoms ...'. Or it might not.

It could be argued that such parents (and children) have a human right to EHE discovery on these grounds of what could emerge, and should be afforded a protected and recognised right to explore possibilities that schooling did not succeed in developing. At present, not only are they assumed to not have a right to EHE, but the idea that they might is ignored and even vilified due to their history of institutional and social non-compliance. Is this fair, democratic and responsible to such individuals? In other words, where human rights protect education and knowing about education, should that protection extend to knowing about *all forms* of education and all people, independent of circumstances?

Given that some forms of education operate according to different timetables of emergent development than others, the issue is especially not clear when various modality options emerge. Presently levels of such subtlety are missing from rights discussions relating to education. Extant research shows that a 'turn-around' from excuse discovery to a genuine interest that could translate into happy and appropriate home education is a journey that does and can occur. Identity and knowledge within EHE practice can evolve (Safran, 2008; Parsons and Lewis, 2010).

In other European countries the idea of a human right to discover EHE (and often also other alternatives to the mainstream) is utterly ignored and/or denied. Germany – and perhaps also now Sweden with recent introduction of new legislation – are European democracies where a 'human right' to discover (and practise) EHE is an especially problematic question (Villalba, 2009; Reimer, 2010; Pattison, 2013; Thomas, 2013). A right to discover EHE without the possibility of practice is not a right but an emptiness and a frustration, highlighting vastly different educational strategies, politics and backgrounds of various nations. Of course it also shows how education is *used* by particular states, including the possibility of negation of personal and individual choice in that equation.

Questions abound: who has the right to decide how, when and why discovery of EHE (and other alternatives away from the 'democratically' constructed mainstream of provision) is acceptable? For instance, can a parent who cannot read home educate? The theory of autonomous EHE says yes. This is so on the basis that learning is not primarily through the parents but through the volition and curiosity of the child, practically supported and facilitated by the parent's care, not educational status (see Thomas and Pattison, 2007, Bergeron, 2009; Safran, 2012). Can a differently abled, blind or deaf parent home educate? Can a single parent home educate, with the lack of social economic contribution that might entail? Can a Nazi home educate? Is a right to EHE (which entails first discovery), practical in a current territory of education seen as a singular mode of the school paradigm? But then what happens to the very idea of democracy if the UN declaration involving a right to education is determined and constrained at the level of modality?

This complicated terrain relates to questions and debates outside of education, forming a part of education demanding new theoretical foundations and 'rules of the game'. The questions highlight how undeveloped our theories of education are at present – how they fit and suit only a certain set of questions. How they demand a certain kind of thinking, logic and communication, including rigid and limiting forms of academic educational discourse. Education becomes in a new multi-modal terrain – *which is a challenge to the current status quo* – not a matter of just a human right to learning and teaching but of a human right also to unlearning, de-schooling, no-teaching and all the benefits that can ensue from 'forgetting' (Smith, 1998; Chokr, 2009). This is a 'mu education'.

Mu education

'Mu' is a Japanese word used in Zen koan philosophy. It is an undoing of assumptions when uttered; a cancellation of a question expecting a straightforward answer. It captures the paradoxical nature of education without schools: it is this *but* also not this and demands, simultaneous to any definitions, that we allow a 'why define it?' also. To define without paradox is not true to what is the case in the alternative educational area. Conroy has touched upon this with his important theory of liminal educational spaces and moments (Conroy, 2004). Not knowing, not defining, applies to an *other* paradigm of education where new and fruitful possibilities reside (see Conroy et al, 2010).

Such ideas connect to this book where 'education', as hegemonically conflated with the idea of mainstream schooling, is not applicable. The result is a term that is both education but also not education as we know it or indeed perhaps can ever know it. It is a form of becoming through being educated that goes against a foreclosed and foreclosing understanding of education (as schooling), reformulating our understanding of education. It becomes something more open because the dominance of schooling as education has been undermined. Or rather, in less nihilistic terms, another way is set forth. Our minds are opened to the potential of education as more and as other than the school: beyond the school. This is not just the claim that education should not be conflated with schooling but the possibility that education doesn't make schooled sense and yet can still be educationally sense-full in the positivity and possibilities inherent in its senselessness.

This 'right of way' is one more in tune with holistic thinking of the east than the analytical linear thinking of the west. EHE as pedagogical/heutagogic practice is holistically inclined. Its philosophy is thus inevitably holistic. We see here then an astonishingly powerful difference between schooling supported by linear and analytic thought and EHE as practice, in that each thinks, sees and acts differently. Many commentators support such a distinction as influential, difficult to reconcile and impactful (Kalamaras, 1994; Olsen, 2000; Nisbett, 2005; Hart, 2004). Yet, valuing this difference offered by alternatives is educationally important. Without it we are half what we could be.

According to Flint and Peim we are foreclosed, captured and enmeshed at intimate levels of self experience in a monolithic technology of education (Flint and Peim, 2012). The technology bears the imprint of an epistemology that is analytic, linear and male (Pendlebury, 2005; Roland Martin, 2011). This exclusionary tendency could also be seen to be part of any project determining human nature, including a human rights agenda. A 'mu' quality is a way for such lineage to become derailed; possibly with surprising and worthwhile benefits. Discovering education *without* schools is a radical mu moment of such a kind. This is why it goes to the heart of everything, as mentioned earlier. A rights agenda then is not really the issue. It is more a case of living freely and being *enabled* to discover the option of an alternative education. Rights only come in to try and protect such freedom.

A right to mu as the educational answer

Mu education relates here to a thesis of this book that discovery of EHE is a discovery away from the world of education (as schooling) we assume will be discovered (in the form of this or that school option). It is a shift – a necessary 'shift', according to Ken Robinson (2010) – into a new educational world. Movement occurs through a 'gateless gate' (see Chapter Four). Discovery of a fixed socialised kind determined by current provision of school choice literature from a local authority, when a child reaches school age, belongs to an easy binary logic: 'child of school age = school attendance'. This is set aside. In educational discovery terms the binary mentioned translates as 'education = being at school'. Contrary and other from this binary is a non-binary or 'fuzzy' logic which makes no sense according to the binary premises of logic: discovering that schooling is not education and that home education is possible. A switch has occurred away from any form of *dominant* logic: 'child of school age = ?'; 'education = ?'.

Such an approach is a 'tree-less' 'logic' (Deleuze and Guattari, 2004), attributable to the epistemological and ontological premises of any form of education that does not coerce towards something predetermined (such as full-time school attendance). This falls into the logic relevant to education Gert Biesta identifies as a 'methodology' of Jacques Rancière. This offers *real* emancipation rather than dependence on the idea of it, by writing which 'itself tries to avoid a position of mastery' (Biesta, 2010, p 41). Do parents, as responsible in law for their child's education, have a right to experience a pathway forward without masters or assumption of needing to be masterly? Is there something fundamentally wrong about this? Might there be something right about a journey and a way of thinking where not wishing to be a master, follow a master or perpetuate such a dynamic in the world is sought for? There are positive gender equality implications furthermore, in doing without 'the master'.

Passing through a gate of discovery of EHE is possible. There is a vague picture that something is happening. Despite a sudden shift being present in discovery, discovery is also much larger: it is a journey with continual forms of curiosity and discovery elements.

In outlining this diffusiveness as important I move another step forward towards how things really occur when education (as multi-modal) takes place. Previously in this book binaries of the mainstream were set up to be against, opposed or opposite to the alternatives. Opposition and its resistance helps encounter with otherness. However, crucially for an appropriate perception of EHE and its value as discovery and then practices for education, a lack of such logic is finally required. We need to 'see the world aright'; to 'throw away the ladder', once we have climbed up – as Ludwig Wittgenstein says in relation to the role of language in gaining an understanding of the world that is more holistically sound, rather than limited and ethically so (Wittgenstein, 2001, p 89). A more ethical educational perspective does not rely on propositional formulation.

As Zen philosophy suggests, a person cannot move forward burdened and conditioned by their previous knowledge. They are required to let go of what they think they know and be open to the infinite possibilities of existence that not knowing allows a person. This is encapsulated in the following ancient Zen koan:

> Joshu asked the teacher Nansen, 'What is the True Way?'
> Nansen answered, 'Every way is the true Way.'
> Joshu asked, 'Can I study it?'
> Nansen answered, 'The more you study, the further from the Way.'
> Joshu asked, 'If I don't study it, how can I know it?'
> Nansen answered, 'The way does not belong to things seen: nor to things unseen. It does not belong to things known: nor to things unknown. Do not seek it, study it, or name it. To find yourself on it, open yourself wide as the sky.'

The idea as it applies to being and becoming emerging from educational practice, is that what is sedimented (in society or people's minds) as a correct way, may be wrong. It may be completely wrong or it may be wrong for some people some of the time. Not knowing – in contrast to the exegesis of the school 'text' that knowing is success – is a pathway forward that can result in new knowing rather than ignorance. Not knowing schooling as education or that schooling is the 'right' form of education, can be fruitful.

It is this *difference* of a way of thinking, with its challenge to an assumption that schooling is the answer, that home educators seem to value. Those who seek for new, emergent, spontaneous, flexible ways for their children to learn are unlikely to find it in institutions bound to function systematically via set curricula. They may find it in EHE. Offering and telling about only schooling when other possibilities also exist, is to *enforce* a particular manner and experience on people: a set epistemology and ontology. There is a debate to be had about the *responsibility* of our politics and our systems to open themselves educationally to more than just the school.

The future of school exit

Will school exit continue to be enacted under strain? Probably not. The world is fast changing (Giddens, 2000) and with the continuing rise of technology will continue to do so. With it come a number of challenges. Key to the present discussion of discovery of alternatives to schooling is the idea that the 'enthralled'-to-the-school mindset (Robinson, 2010) that once expected and accepted mainstream schools as education, might be itself changing along with global developments. Whilst the loss of the school, if it is possible to have a democratic and socially open form, is bemoaned (Fielding and Moss, 2011), schooling as an institution of any kind is perhaps coming to an end.

There is a now a trend in tune with the idea of people educationally 'doing it for themselves' which is termed by some 'co-production' – a phrase coined to capture new ways in which various social phenomenon are operating (nef, 2008; Boyle and Harris, 2009). Co-production is seen as having emerged as a way for public services to function and as also a new mentality.

This sensibility for self-regulated control can be seen in varying sectors: television shows which demand and receive audience vote-in participation (and with the digital technology to facilitate this), thereby actively change the nature of the show (Harkin, 2008; Lawson, 2008); media articles published online solicit reader comments; the proliferation of blogs, wikis and websites; the use of 'people power' to design products (Sample, 2007); personal 'in control' budget schemes for healthcare or elderly care (Revill, 2007; Gould, 2008); even devices designed to operate and function off the physical movements of individuals such as their heartbeat or dance movements, using these to create kinetic power (McKie, 2008). The ways in which individuals are being asked to be self-empowered are growing, albeit with the possibility of criticisms that such 'empowerment' is in fact the off-loading of labour costs onto individuals.

In other ways people are feeling that their voice matters and can have effect. Activism, or people taking action into their own hands, is gaining ground (Vidal, 2007). Member-led (often online) organisations rally to ensure that other 'ordinary' people stand up for their beliefs with collective action; a method which is proving effective (Puckett, 2011).

As one pertinent example, in the wake of the Badman Report and fears of its implementation, a group of home educators demonstrated publically with a protest march in London in September 2009 (Sugden, 2009). As previously mentioned, home educators are well known for being able to collectively act on behalf of their rights, even if doing so is controversial for others (Stevens, 2003a). Less happily perhaps but not in denial of the phenomenon – the 2011 UK riots were organised via online and mobile phone messaging (Ball and Brown, 2011). People are not just doing it for themselves, they are also capable of organising themselves in opposition to those who previously thought they had full control.

Educational implications from these social developments abound. The Conservative party, in the run-up to the 2010 election, promised as part of their election manifesto that they would make provision for 'Free schools' that parents could start with state funding should those parents decide there was a need. Now 'studio schools' funded by enterprise are beginning to emerge (Department for Education, 2012). Discussion of the politics of such specific (conservative, not socialist) economic initiatives is outside the scope of this book. What it does show is that diversity (of a kind) can flourish if it is *enabled* to occur. So it is strange that enabling home education meets with such a resolute hands-off approach from the very same powers who are offering difference and diversity of schooling models (House of Commons Education Committee, 2013). Again, I point to a limited educational vision which *just doesn't go far enough* for the world we are moving into.

Government versions of education stipulate the vision the public lives with, yet with the rise of the internet and mobile technology it is possible to observe significant changes in attitudes to education. Because of the internet, economies alter (see for example Copenhagen Futures Institute, 2009) and this affects how we can live, learn and become (Bonk, 2009). The impact of the internet is seen in new forms of web-based education such as virtual schools through home computers (Harris, 2007) and new technology experiments with virtual worlds creating dedicated educational 'islands' in Web 2.0 environments such as Second Life, where old rules of desks, chalk and talk and top-down hierarchies of power do not apply (Twining, 2007). Children have taught themselves even advanced tasks using a 'hole in the wall' internet portal (Mitra et al, 2005). Technology is changing how education functions (see Waks, 2012 for further details).

Small private schools are mushrooming with economic models that parents on the lowest of the world's wages can afford (Tooley, 2009; Srivastava, 2013). Social pioneers of difference are delivering learning opportunities outside of formal school registration in slums and rural backwaters where the mainstream does not reach (Leadbetter and Wong, 2010). Enterprise is using mobile phone technology and TV entertainment to deliver cheap learning for specified ends, such as proficiency in English in developing countries (Bunz, 2010). New business modelling allows free access to educational resources, as we see now with universities making their lectures freely accessible on the web via Massive Online Open Courses (MOOCs) (Parr, 2013). Attending the institution becomes optional – at least for interaction with some knowledge content (Adenekan, 2007).

All of this has potential at least to enhance the dialogic for and in education. Yet the dialogic struggles *in* schools. A recent drive to promote school councils – as a democratic attempt – is problematic and incomplete as democratic 'style', requiring deep thought yet to materialise as actual and successful democracy in schooling (Trafford, 2003; Harber, 2009a). Naturally if such developments remain tokenistic they will be disappointing and fall short of modern educational needs in line with changes happening at a fast pace, as briefly outlined above. Increased openness to open learning and enjoyment of the dialogic that it may be able to develop, will inevitably bring some kind of inevitable better understanding of what happens educationally outside and without schools.

Does technology facilitate exit from schooling?

In terms of the special role of the internet in discovering EHE it is clear that the thousands of web blogs, wikis, websites and forums discussing EHE play a role. Many people mention 'googling' home education, as with the following interview extracts from the study informing this book:

> **Lynn:** ... I actually put the words 'education otherwise' into Google ... but I didn't know any ... I didn't know it was an option really. I wasn't aware consciously of it being an option but somewhere subconsciously I'd heard it. So I put 'education otherwise' into the search engine and up came that page and I knew I'd got the answer ... When it said [*excited*] when it said 'Education Otherwise' home education, I was like 'wooooooarrh I've got it got it! I've bloody found the answer!' I knew. There was never a second of doubt that they were coming out of school, you know ... (July 2009)

Sorena: ... and I can't quite remember how I came about the whole idea of home education but I remember just doing a search on the internet and doing home education in Google or whatever it was and I came up with various sites – probably Education Otherwise and all the common ones, all the typical ones, and all it said was it's legal and that's what I needed. I didn't need to be told anything more ... (July 2009)

Family H, Mother: We joked, oh we're home educating you ...What happened was I was joking about it and I went to Amazon and put home education in and Alan Thomas's book came up and I just read the review, said most of it is done conversationally, and I thought to myself: 'That's what we do anyway' ... (July 2009)

Samantha: I suppose I became interested – I've got a computer so I read various blogs – and I become interested in Montessori, Steiner, Waldorf and then various blogs of people who were home schooling or unschooling and it just seemed like a wonderful thing to do. That's ... that would be my dream. (September 2009)

Nina: I asked several people on the internet and the internet is really good for that because you can go on all the yahoo groups for the different home education locations ... (July 2009)

Sophia: The ones who stay [*with EHE*] are the ones who don't labour to get informed [*via EHE charities*] as they are already committed in deeper ways ...There is less reason to stay as a member of a home education support organisation if you are tapped into everything that is happening anyway, i.e. if you are on the internet all the time. (May 2010)

In the lives of home educating families, one study on support for home educators found that the internet played a large role (Atkinson et al, 2007) and there is recognition in the history of EHE in the US of the internet's role in the rise in numbers (Gaither, 2008) as well as understanding of the internet as a facilitator of networks (Apple, 2007).

No research yet has focused specifically on the development of the internet as involved in a rise of EHE numbers or of discovery of EHE via the internet. Anecdotal evidence for this correlation abounds in casual comments in various home education website blogs, threads and other discussion spaces. Proof of such a tendency to inform about education through internet resources can be seen all over the World Wide Web. An example of the kind of rationale that informs this trend is given here:

> New technology and rapid globalization have changed the way we think and act as individuals. As the power of the Internet grows, our ability to conduct research and to educate ourselves becomes more meaningful. Students worldwide are taking advantage of the resources available and using the information to mould the future success of their personal, academic and working lives ... (www.applyesl.com, 2010)

Mass access to web-based information blossoming in England from 2000 onwards coincides with the proliferation of articles on the 'phenomenon' of home education: more articles appeared discussing home education from 2003/04 onwards than ever before. It is a too tenuous link, given a present lack of research, to claim correlation between the rise in media articles (reporting the newsworthy phenomenon of rising numbers) and the wide emergence of the internet at the start of the twenty-first century with regards to consideration of EHE discovery. Yet there is no doubt that internet usage and the discovery of EHE have a relationship. This relationship is seen here as a combination of a lack of active EHE-appropriate (that is, not disappointing in its legal, philosophical or educational accuracy) information provision by government and a new social trend towards people 'doing it for themselves', empowered by technological change. The internet facilitates school exit. It is perfect for people actively and constantly searching for new and updated ways of doing things.

Discovery as an elitist privilege?

There are issues with even this 'freedom' to discover EHE and a possible human right to exit schooling. It is not equally distributed even if, as an 'informal' human right, it might be theoretically an entitlement of all people. The issues of discovery here are mostly linked to cultural and social capital. The EHE charity member below describes how many people calling their helpline not only do not have good internet access, but more importantly have never received educational input suitable to be able to do the most basic of internet functions such as using a common internet search engine:

> **Sophia:** We have a lot of people making inquiries who don't have access to the internet ... don't know how to Google ... (April 2010)

In conversation with a local authority educational psychologist (personal communication, November 2012) who had been part of a team visiting (monitoring) EHE families, he suggested to me that there are children who get better educational provision than others. This seemed to him to be linked to high or low levels of cultural capital. In some respects this must be true. However, one must question the role of cultural capital in inculcating certain expectations about what a suitable and efficient education is and the middle-class blinkers that tribalism for the value of culture can create. Quite simply: Whose culture? What for? Whose opinion? (see Gribble, 2012, de Oliveira, 2012, Macfarlane, 2012).

This then turns us back to the idea of a right to discover education without schools. Is discovery of EHE a privilege, not a right or an opportunity, because of issues connected to social, economic and cultural capital? Even down to basic knowledge of how to use a web-based search engine? Education as schooling is universally available in the UK; education without schooling is not because of knowledge acquisition differences only. Apart from operational issues such as parental work commitments, and so on, the *prima facie* reasons for this would appear to be issues connected to inequality in *opportunity* of discovery. This is reflected in the data, especially in the street survey as discussed in Chapter Two.

Much has been said directly or indirectly about the reproduction of social inequality in and through a mainstream school setting (for example Bourdieu and Passeron, 1990; McCulloch, 1998; Reay, 2001). What has not yet been adequately addressed in educational literature is the vast territory of inequality that permeates the choice towards alternative educational modes and educational equality outside and unlinked to any schooling system. Paula Rothermel's research suggested working class parents make up approximately 15–20% of all home educators (Rothermel 2002; Rothermel 2003). Yet, there is still a disparity in discovery between 'classes', according to the street survey data (see Lees, 2011a). This needs further research because it suggests a deeply unfair situation.

Little is currently known about differentials in long-term outcomes for different socio-economic backgrounds in and through EHE, although there are indications that differentials are smaller in home education (Rothermel, 2002) than in school provision, where disparities in achievement unfortunately match background: with the working class and disadvantaged coming off worst (Goodman and Gregg, 2010).

Differences in levels of discovery between class groups appear to be linked to levels of cultural capital, at a deep level of inequality. Superficially, the various avenues of discovery of EHE showed that it is happening through broadsheets read by those supposedly high in cultural capital as well as women's tabloid-style magazines for those whose cultural capital is apparently more limited. The *deep* level disparity is shown in the street survey data, which shows a strong bias towards affluent-looking participants having greater levels of awareness and knowledge compared to less affluent-looking participants.[1] That data indicated there was a great deal of interest amongst the less affluent participants to know more about EHE as an educational option and strong, common vocalisation amongst them of a desire to be told more by educational authorities.

What has also emerged from my personal experience talking socially to various people about my research over a number of years and more importantly, the street survey data, is a marked tendency for some affluent people to think and feel that poorer people should not know that EHE is an option. The reasons they give are generally that 'such' people would not do a good job and the language they use is disparaging of the ability of 'such' people to be 'qualified'. This is a disturbing finding, which not only bears out signs of strong classist attitudes in society with regard to educational options, such as those highlighted by McCulloch (1998) and Willis (1981), but that these attitudes are still working against less affluent people even *outside* schooling as a concept. The result is that discovering EHE is rarer for this group than for more affluent people. If we are linking class to affluence, as is often done in the UK, is it a social class secret that children don't have to go to school? Education without schools presents equality issues.

The fact that some affluent participants' attitude was to not share information about EHE awareness, shows that keeping discovery of EHE on an informal, word-of-mouth basis is a class issue – a have-and-have-nots divide – requiring redress through democratically minded equality of opportunity for discovery, reflected in governmental policy. Given that the UN Universal Declaration of Human Rights is for human beings irrespective of class or financial status, with the emphasis therein in Article 26(3) stating that (*all*) 'Parents have a prior right to

choose the kind of education that shall be given to their children'
(United Nations, 1948), class tensions in England around who should
or should not know that EHE is a valid and legal option for the
education of children, suggests a government failure. There needs to
be more *active* government-provided publicity towards the discovery of
the concept of modal educational options to ease this injustice. If this
does not occur, educational inequality, beyond and without schooling,
is likely to persist unchallenged.

Conclusion

Children of school age are leaving schools and they are entitled to
do so. Information regarding this, ability to do this and the structural
knowledge background required to enable a concept of educational
difference to be understood are all interdependent. Education without
schools is a territory of chance, luck, privilege, migration, rights and
wrongs. It lies at the heart of what is wrong with schools and possibly
also at the heart of what is right about education; that exit continues to
involve educational interest. Because it is about going against the grain,
school exit demands volition and courage. Education without schools
is not for the cowardly. It seems also counterintuitive for those arguing
for a basic right to education. Given 'the fragile state of education as
a human right' around the world in many areas (Tomasevski, 2005, p
208), to try and understand education specifically without schools as
a human right is not only complicated but difficult. School exit and
alternatives, seems in this sense to be a luxury for those in affluent
countries who eschew the basics that others fight hard to achieve.

Whether education is with or without schooling, the current system
for understanding educational rights is inadequately structured (see
Tomasevski, 2003). Modality options of difference ought to form part
of an emerging and struggling picture of educational (and human)
rights. The reason for embracing educational difference in the issue of
such rights lies with the failures of education in schools. Alternatives
enable promises of the idea of education for human flourishing that
state-provided schooling continues to fail to provide by denying many
other basic human rights, such as that of not being harmed (Harber,
2004). Such a line of argument opens up education to the market; to
non-educational aspects of the educational system in ways that might
show educational promise (Tooley, 2009; Srivastava, 2013) rather than
necessarily peril. After all: 'There are no straightforward paradigms to
be applied nor any simple positions from which "privatisations" can be
viewed' (Ball, 2007, p 185). The ideal, of course, is for freely provided

educational provision to embrace *alternative* promise, and quickly, before so many (rightly) leave schools, and the possibilities for social justice of public schooling are substantially undermined.

Note

[1] See the original study http://etheses.bham.ac.uk/1570/1/Lees11PhD.pdf for impressions of class background in the street survey field notes, as made from the researcher's own positionality.

EIGHT

Understanding discovery differences

> ... professionals who work with parents should address them not just as pawns in the system that can be steered by technical reason, but – very differently – as people who are capable of independent practical judgement. (Smedts, 2008, p 122)

Introduction

As previous chapters have attempted to outline, discovering EHE sits within a maelstrom of issues and whilst it can occur simply – in a moment – it also drags some complicated factors into the lives of those involved. These factors are linked to social, political, educational, familial and parenting matters.

What I offer in this chapter is a way through the discovery thicket: a framework for discovery so that those who have a genuine desire to home educate can be left to educate according to the wonderful journey, philosophies, practices and developments possible in this alternative modality. A framework is offered because not all discovery is genuine and professionals seem to be in need of conceptual boundaries marking what is to the non-practitioner, unfamiliar and seemingly worrying territory.

The ethics of the framework rests very much with the above quotation: parents ought to be trusted to get on with the job. Whilst that may sound counterintuitive for those who are aware of the unfortunately too many seriously abusive parents (one being too many) in society, I suggest that when it comes to home education, trust of parents is a key site of democratic social expression. All parents – independent of means, education, socio-economic category – have a right to home educate. They also have a right to discover home education; come upon its difference, growing slowly into its educational offering which is being given as a positive to both child *and* parent.

To go against this freedom is to succumb to a disgust of the dignity of parenting, evolution in the family and to deny elements of heutagogical growth through the freedoms of the practices inherent in autonomous EHE that enable the child to live well. It is to forget the parent is important. A wish to control these intuitive and emergent relationships takes away value for the role that parents have in relation to their children. The only way in which I feel that this strong stance underpinning the framework presented here can be taken is by virtue of the fact that *non-genuine* home educators are few and also very easy to understand as not practicing EHE. Therefore trusting home educators is easy. It definitely ought to be the default.

This chapter's discussion has policy implications because it offers to local authorities something which they are currently missing: a framework for analysing EHE practice as legally carried out and appropriate. By applying the framework discussed below, a need for changes to the current status of the law in relation to EHE is avoided. *Differences in discovery* matter for all aspects of what is currently problematic for EHE legality and official action in this regard. A tri-partite framework is now outlined of 'negative', 'excuse' and 'genuine' discovery.

Negative discovery

There is growing awareness of certain specific and deeply unfortunate situations involving discovery of EHE as negative. This book focuses on data and discussion highlighting positive discovery. This positivity is occurring within positive scenarios: families who care for one another; people who are relatively physically healthy, reasonably mentally well and perhaps without disabling financial problems. Yet this is not the only story. Isolated instances have occurred where EHE has suffered in the media spotlight when the situation was negative discovery.

The *Khyra Ishaq* case in Birmingham, UK,[1] saw media attention focused on EHE during the period 2008–10 (Glendinning, 2008; Radford, 2010). The conflation of this case's circumstances with an educational situation called 'elective home education' is, as we will see, false. It had nothing to do with EHE. But it did involve *negative discovery* of EHE.

In this case, home education was consistently reputed to be a factor contributing to a young girl's death by neglect. The partner of the child's mother discovered that home education meant in law that children did not have to attend school and that unwelcome visits into the home (or sight of the child) from inspecting EHE officers were also prohibited. Seemingly, he passed this information on to the mother (Radford, 2010, p 53) who chose to verbally state to the school and others that she was home educating her children. It does appear that she did not actually directly deregister her children from the school, but unusually instead did so in a letter to the Special Educational Needs Assessment Service (Radford, 2010, p 52). This negative discovery caused conflation of EHE with the neglect.

When the home education of the Ishaq children was inspected by the Birmingham 'education otherwise'[2] inspection team for regulation of EHE practice, a show of books and a room arranged to look like a schoolroom seems to have been enough for the inspection team to agree that an appropriate education was taking place and thus that the children were well. This judgement was subsequently criticised in the Serious Case Review as a lack of 'professional curiosity' (Radford, 2010, p 58). This meant that safeguarding procedures were not developed by social workers *unrelated* to education. A further shocking safeguarding case including a home education claim, which emerges as this book goes to print, looks likely to show another instance of a lack of professional curiosity about child welfare (Davies, 2013).

Without going further into the *Ishaq* case, which is outside of this book's remit, a certain lack stands out: EHE was not judged to be *actively* practiced. There was no show of curiosity on the part of the children for learning, nor evidence of active facilitation by the parents for that learning. This is all that is needed for us to know that EHE is in motion, but here it was lacking. The picture was still. As Rothermel points out, triangulating proof (if there is concern for welfare) is the mark of effective home education (Rothermel, 2010): action (such as a trip to see something new), connections to action (souvenirs from the trip) and conversation linked to action (discussion of the trip and the materials gathered). A *moving*, vibrant, socially inclined educational picture is the sign of the alternative modality positively enabled (Hern, 2008).

There was no evidence to this effect in the *Ishaq* scenario. Thus, the involvement of EHE in this case of neglect was by virtue of *discovery alone*. The discovery of EHE was not discovery in the profound sense of a life event and a journey into another world of education and lifestyle, involving active practices. Invocation of the term and use of the label of EHE practice was a falsifying move. EHE was not taking place. It played no part in the situation.

Instead what occurred was an extreme and dark form of manipulation of a system to allow parents/guardians to act with lack of care for and abuse of the children for whom they had responsibility. For Khyra Ishaq, being noted by authorities as a home educated child was her death warrant but this had nothing to do with EHE practice because various procedures were not correctly followed, which as Rothermel points out, is what leads to negative portrayals of EHE (Rothermel, 2010).

Furthermore, active practice can be judged from parents. If asked, the parent-guardians of Khyra Ishaq would have had no opinions or developing knowledge about EHE. But they were meant to have that knowledge as home educators. There was almost no need to look at the child's 'experiences' of books, writing, toys or whatever. If pressed, those parental carers would have had little enthusiasm or interest in the idea of joining the local community EHE network, understanding educational philosophies and styles, reading about EHE practice, seeking out other children and parents to socialise with or going on trips to look at, for instance, steam engines or to the butterfly museum. As Sophie suggested in Chapter Seven, genuine EHE parents are 'tapped into everything that is happening'. Safran describes what I call 'genuine' EHE parents as participating within 'communities of practice,' even if this is at first in a minor or peripheral way (2010). Whilst these things are not necessary for all home educators, they are each a possibility and highly likely in EHE. A *total* lack of such active engagement with what EHE can involve is a starting point from which to question parents further about what education means to them. In other words, getting educationally philosophical with parents is important in understanding how EHE is occurring.

The *Ishaq* case was of discovery that *related solely to the legal framework* connected to EHE practising status. It was taking advantage of this framework whilst doing nothing real. So, in the Khyra Ishaq story, *no real aspects* of EHE practice have come out of the coverage of this case.

Despite strong ties to EHE being implied in both the Serious Case Review (Radford, 2010), the High Court judgment and various media reports (for example Shepherd, 2010a), this case was about an abuse of the law for the sake of perpetrating child abuse. Linking it to EHE is a misjudgement of the facts allowed only by ignorance of EHE (see Thomas and Pattison, 2010) and, I suggest, educationism also.

In the context of this book's consideration of discovery of EHE as a personal event in the self, this negative discovery situation is outside of what discovery of EHE means as a joyful or 'saving' event. Negative discovery is a rare non-event, which is most often a deliberate and sad cover for crime.

Excuse discovery

Such dark discovery aside, it can be noticed that there is a less sinister form of discovery which is an *excuse*. This is where parents realise *a claim* of EHE practice is a way to avoid fines and threats of imprisonment if children are not attending school. But like negative discovery, this excuse is unlikely to show signs of educational action; at least not at first.

Coming upon home education as an excuse can happen serendipitously just like the negative example above: through word of mouth, a TV programme, internet forums and print media coverage. But what is focused on by parents is not testimonies of interesting, stimulating educational opportunities but instead the fact of the freedom from school attendance.

Parents can legally claim EHE and deregister their children from school when they are being challenged by an Education Welfare Officer (EWO). As discussed in the previous chapter, some are even offered information about EHE by headteachers as an 'option' away from schooling if their children are deemed to be a troubling force in the school. It has been noticed that a pre-typed deregistration form, from schooling into EHE status, was provided by a council official to parents of persistent truants (BBC News online, 2007).

Normal practice is that an EWO can and does suggest to certain parents with children out of school for truancy, or in the case of Travellers potentially paid work (Bhopal and Myers, 2009), that unless they send or ensure their children go to school, they will personally face consequences through fines and possible imprisonment. Such parents can instantly claim EHE practice with a letter to their child's school. It might seem as though the legal 'loophole' that applied in the *Ishaq* case to allow avoidance of contact with such officials is being invoked. Parents who claim that home education is being undertaken create a set of legalities applicable to them, different from a parent's child-truancy relationship with the Education Welfare Service (EWS). Thus, with an EHE practice claim parents can enjoy legal protection for what was previously considered truancy. They need henceforth only be concerned with home education inspection, which is on the whole minimal in comparison to the fines and threat of prison associated with persistent truancy, and open to various discussable interpretations and time lags (such as months of recovery from schooling trauma), whereas a school attendance compliance order is clear cut and fairly swift in delivery.

A claim of EHE via deregistration, as the Badman Review (2009) highlighted, makes it more difficult for authorities to navigate persecution of parents of truants. We see perhaps in the existence of excuse discovery of EHE, a clearer picture of why the law regarding home education has been sought to be tightened.

Yet understanding excuse discovery is not simple because it is different from negative discovery. Whereas the previous category involves crime that forecloses the possibility of EHE becoming active practice (because the situation is too criminal for education to get a look in), excuse discovery is a reaction to a difficult situation caused invariably from outside the family: truancy, school disaffection, bullying and consequent absenteeism, and so on.

It might be that inadvertent and initially disinterested discovery starts as a reactive excuse in the face of threats from the EWO. Yet, it could develop into a good idea taken seriously. If it doesn't develop as active EHE practice, then it is negative according to the framework of compulsory education law.

Defending *the fair and equal right* of all parents to claim home education status (via formal deregistration) is important. What happens next should legitimately be practice of EHE, rather than something dark in intent as in negative discovery described above, but practice of EHE can begin as a journey which takes time to gear up to full-blown identity (Safran, 2008; Morton, 2010a; Safran; 2010). The option and choice for EHE can occur at any point in the life of a child and their parents, even in circumstances where they are coming up against the authorities because schooling is not working out. Persecution and denial of the EHE option in circumstances of truancy would be both illegal and inappropriate, despite the start possibly being merely an excuse. Those claiming EHE in this way need to urgently take EHE seriously, if they are to avoid their discovery becoming a crime and an unreal invocation of EHE as legal practice.

As mentioned previously, sometimes schooling is something that one might wish to escape by any means *legal*. It has a difficult nature capable of including violences without adequate measures of control or remedy (Block, 1997; Yoneyama, 1999; Harber, 2009b; Olson, 2009). A bad scenario at a school and involvement with the EWS might begin awareness of educational pathways and choice without school as a positive avenue to pursue. Who ought or can judge and hinder such a journey, if actively pursued? Suggesting EHE as a legal alternative to fines and prison is not a bad idea. Strong initial monitoring for development of educational activity might be a reasonable price for parents to pay in such cases (only) to be able to find a way out of court appearances and disentanglement from the EWS.

Genuine discovery

According to the framework of discovery offered by this book, genuine discovery involves a transformation to some degree of the person who experiences it. That transformation might be sudden and a form of éclat, or it might emerge slowly with EHE practice. However, at some point discovery of EHE as educational difference will involve a conclusive moment of realisation of that otherness, involving intimations of its possibilities. Its difference from schooling is personally and educationally transformative (Lees, 2011c).

In the present discussion I focus on the first moment of discovery as a technical understanding of the possibility of EHE in the UK as legal and done by others: as possible. Involved in this moment is a need: an interest in practising EHE in the family is required. Otherwise realisation of the legality alone is superficial. According to the framework I offer, superficial awareness is not discovery of EHE, which is a profound event moment.

Without practice, transformation is limited, likely to stall and wither. In such a situation, EHE is unlikely to be different from 'a school at home'. EHE practised is not of an unyielding schooling mentality. It is, as outlined previously in Chapter Two, often different from mainstream schooling practice in its autonomous-tending form; likely to develop with time and adjustments as well as relaxation of any previously strictly held notions of what education can be. Being at home or educating from the home develops autonomy as an underpinning rationale, even if what is then possibly *chosen* is a formal structure for learning goals. A home is unlikely to be able or want to replicate the institution of a school.

Also, transformation through genuine discovery is positive in some manner – welcomed and creating enthusiasm (Lees, 2011a). Holistically affecting, it touches the whole person on a number of levels. Discovery is a precursor to a 'fundamental change in lifestyle' (Neuman and Avriam, 2003) which is impactful; demanding changes tantamount to sets of sacrifices (financial, time-wise, energy, approbation of friends and family). Such is genuine discovery: active educational practice tending towards difference from schooling, positive discoveries of self and other, commitment to an educational pathway that has the effect and/or possibilities of transforming lifestyle and world views over time.

Discovery occurs by chance in the present educational climate. This is because of a lack of information *promoted* by state information providers to appear in the public domain. As mentioned before, the pathway of genuine home education discovery is not easy. It is not mainstream practice and is a negation of the normal and the normalising. Indeed, it does not happen to everyone, being a form of tipping point into a *sought, wished for* difference. This is so even if, as above, I highlight the right of all adults with legal responsibility for their children to take up this option if they are sincerely interested (interest developing reasonably quickly) to pursue its practice.

Making distinctions

It is important to make a distinction between different kinds of discovery of EHE. The consequence otherwise is negative press coverage and potentially even policy (Shepherd, 2010a), based on and following ignorance that conflates EHE action with EHE claims. Negative press coverage of EHE as a result of such conflations is damaging and detrimental to this educational option which increasingly proves itself of great value.

Not damaging home educators' reputations and that of home education as practice ought to be as important as the upholding of professional regard for teachers and the reputation of schools. The trouble is, as Graham Stuart MP points out in Chapter Three, home educators have little clout to refute whatever slanderous assertions or mud others care to throw at them. They are 'easily ignored' if maligned and a vulnerable population in contrast to the might of the state; problems mitigated only by acting collectively or having champions in power. This is all time-consuming, complicated and demands a great deal of energy involving collective action and organisation amongst significant diversity.

Where safeguarding is a genuine concern in a family, home *education* should be strongly demarcated as a factor from such matters. Rightly evoked as a signifier, it is active educational practice. Schools are not blamed for the abuse by parents of the children attending them because they are deemed educational places, not primary personal domains. Likewise home education is an *educational* situation despite its location as within a personal domain. It is an educational situation that offers potential for abuse to be hidden if it is abused as an educational signifier, but genuine home educators do not abuse their educational opportunity as home educators. Only child abusers do so. That home education brings the personal close to the educational is a bonus for many genuine home educators, not a sign of abuse. Abuse occurs *under the guise* of the signifier of home education practice.

Without such a profile being understood theoretically and practically in policy, EHE is picked up by 'populist anxieties' (see Conroy, 2010) as a site of potential abuse of children. The astonishing innuendo to which, in particular, media coverage of EHE has resorted at times is disturbing. One example of the media leading the public into prejudice and bias against EHE will suffice amongst many available to quote:

> Labour proposed a system of registration to monitor home schooling, which affects up to 80,000 children. Parents resisted it, and the Tories sided with them, not kids at potential risk. Education Secretary Michael Gove claimed that registration would 'stigmatise' home educating parents. Not if they're doing the job properly, it wouldn't. What have they got to fear? (Routledge, 2010)

In 2012 the British Prime Minister found himself defending 'gay people' against a 'witch hunt' when he was controversially handed on live television a list of 'suspected' paedophiles by the show's host. He called immediately on air for due process and legal measures alone where strong evidence exists and urged for a cessation to unfair and reputation-damaging speculation. So, what is wrong should be judged *by the law* and not by the public and media sensationalism? (Chapman, 2012). The same applies to home education. There is far too much ignorance about EHE practice for it not to require greater and better information provision and more robust frameworks of understanding, so that it is protected from 'witch hunts'. Anything else is unjust and also democratically stupid.

Conclusion

During the 2009 Badman Review, I witnessed, as a researcher, home education go from being promoted in the media as a joyous possibility to almost overnight becoming vilified and feared. The *Khyra Ishaq* case and other (rare) unfortunate associations with difficult circumstances are often cited as a reason why EHE needs regulation and tight controls. At no point in the response to headline grabbing drama was it pointed out that EHE is *educational* practice. This is shocking ignorance and educationism.

A framework of identifying motivations for EHE practice at the point of discovery can be useful to better identify the benefits and genuine educational nature of EHE. It will sort the wheat from the chaff; the non-educational from the educational. Whilst understanding of motivations to home educate exist (Rothermel, 2003; Morton, 2010a), there needs to be understanding of discovery. Without this people enter into EHE, in law, without educational action and this can cause problems for genuine educational practice. A discovery-identifying framework aids in creating a situation where EHE is entered into willingly, in an informed manner and with appropriate support. All of this is currently subject to problematisations, confusions and misinterpretation by some authorities and parents. A standard for educational sincerity at the point of discovery could be judged through signs as follows: is the parent pleased to have discovered education without schools and is this part of curiosity about how it can work, leading to active development of practice?

EHE discovery is not always elective, so any framework has to take that into account. Where non-elective discovery happens, it seems that eventually many such parents adapt and find benefits in EHE practice (Parsons and Lewis, 2010; Wray and Thomas, 2013). Therefore, it cannot be said that being 'forced' into EHE by forms of school failure is necessarily a bad thing for either parents or children. It is involuntary yet could yield solutions to intractable problems that schools consistently and disturbingly fail to adequately address.

The concept of EHE is not common. So it is possible to see easily whether people are making the required effort to familiarise themselves with the difference involved. This is a gradual learning process and cannot happen overnight. Not only is EHE educational for children but it invariably involves educational understanding about another pedagogic/heutagogic way for parents. It is education but it is, fascinatingly, also highly educational regarding education (McKee, 2002; Safran, 2008). It is a sign of genuine EHE in action that the practice itself is a steep learning curve, until well practised.

The framework I offer enables those whose job it is to deal with EHE matters to separate out genuine home educators from difficult and tainting conflations. I very much hope that these conflations stop because, as an academic educationist, what I see from the window of my ivory tower is an important educational landscape for all to explore with rich resources. To place or allow EHE, as education on its own terms, to languish under threat from destructive educationism and ignorance, leads potentially to destruction of educational capital, making us all and educational studies poorer.

Notes

[1] *Birmingham City Council v AG and others* [2009] EWHC 3720 (Fam). The case transcript is available from www.bailii.org.

[2] Not to be confused with the *Education Otherwise* charity, whose remit is EHE support and advocacy.

NINE

Concluding remarks

When it comes to the education of children we have been conditioned as a society to assume that the word education refers primarily to schooling. Discovering that is does not have to, and can refer to something else as full-time practice, is a revelation for many people. They discover new possibilities. In this book I have tried to elucidate some features of home education which are ripe for development. The work here presented is part of a start in this direction and it sits within a rich body of excellent research and commentary on the phenomenon and fact of EHE (see for example and as an overview Kunzman and Gaither, 2013). Further work would inevitably develop understanding of parenting in relation to EHE as education and look at philosophies of care, the feminine, the dynamic of couples as educationists and much more. I see this work usefully done in and through theory and philosophy, but empirical research of a kind that follows a 'gold standard' research approach, according to rules respected by a policy mainstream is also a territory for development.

Despite many excellent features (including legality), the UK shares with perhaps all countries around the world the status of an educational state provider acting prejudicially against EHE. This prejudice is largely tolerated, not significantly contested and causes havoc for many families. In the past it was outright and open prejudice. Now it is, I would suggest, closer to implicit bias – an unconscious prejudice that operates like an open prejudice in its effects. I have called this situation educationism. I hope identifying – as a named concept – bias and prejudice against EHE and other educational alternatives will raise awareness about the limited vision of education we currently have. This vision imposes *limitations* upon society and the upbringing of children. Schooling is not enough for the formation of vibrant citizenry and caring individuals. The value of the home as an educator, and especially when full time, is something to which we need, as a society, to pay much more attention. Although schooling can be loving to a degree, for many it is not loving at all or loving enough. Homes are more likely to be better able to offer and develop love than institutions. It is my belief that the love which can flow in EHE scenarios is an educational tool and an educational good, and renders EHE specialist in terms of its ability to involve love in education and its outcomes.

For countries where EHE is illegal or extremely hard for parents to justify, this *limitation* on what it means to choose educationally and the closure of *diverse* routes to being and becoming that education can afford is shocking. I believe it is also dangerous. It stops options for necessary educational love, and with the various violences that schooling can teach it impoverishes people. They cannot see any other vision available of learning how to live and learn in society, generation after generation.

Reframing how we judge effective EHE practice is useful. It would fruitfully and appropriately be done by focusing not on assessment of the child's education; instead, it should look at the parents' understanding of the educational route they have chosen for their children. A serious and engaged adult *conversation* can occur with interested parties, so these parties can understand the practice. A bit like taking a driving test, but through trust in conversation and without tick boxes. The genuine nature of the educational involvement in EHE can be grasped as a part of a long and developing journey in understanding and working with EHE as an educational modality. This way, the length of time of involvement in EHE – and thus depth of knowledge and engagement – can be taken into account. Those at the start of their journey are unlikely to know much but will show signs of wanting to learn and understand. There will be signs of educational *action*. EHE is not a still image but a moving, morphing event of discovery of the educational in relation to the world.

Those some way along their EHE journey will show signs of complex understanding. It is not even hard or (particularly) ridiculous to tick boxes against such signs: research/reading/internet communication, participating in local groups, outside activities such as swimming club, trips to museums, and so on. A diverse democratically agreed list could be assembled between home educators and local authorities – and even on an individual basis given that conversation is key – that would be easy for adults to rationally accept. EHE families are active anyway. They cannot help but get into such matters. But, whilst making adults tick boxes can be simple, it is hard to create tick-box assessment against learning and education of autonomously educated children.

In this way the nature of autonomous EHE as allowing emergent results, according to readiness, can be given space to manifest over time. This would replace an incompatible school assessment mentality imposed on EHE assessments by officials, which too easily demands results according to age bracket. All EHE parents, families and children form unique dynamics and the various levels of these dynamics create a beautifully rich and complex picture. The picture sustains and strengthens the lost 'notion of parents as people, of the parent–child relationship as constantly developing, in flux and challenging, intersecting with others and other roles' (Suissa, 2006, p 72). It is a picture incompatible with what is expected from education as schooling. Tragically, for many, schooling seems to impoverish the possibility for such a parent-child dynamic (Suissa sees the impoverishment in the modern conception of parenting but doesn't make the necessary criticism of or link to the role of schooling). Impoverishment is, I believe, due to a common issue: the technological enframing that schooling involves (Flint and Peim, 2012) and which some commentators notice in parenthood norms of the current age (Smedts, 2008; Smith, 2010). EHE is educational fresh air, blowing in through the window of all this enframing nonsense.

Educationism can work against EHE practitioners. Without due care and reflexivity it can also operate in educational studies and against academic educationists. It is vital that education as an academic discipline questions its current ability/inability and willingness/reluctance to embrace educational difference in all that it does – from ethics committee decisions, to styles of thought as expressed, or rejected, in writing for journals. There are signs that knowing what education as a broad terrain could mean becomes lost; that one vision is demanded; one way or style of thinking and one modality. Do we all think the same educationally? Do we want to? I hope the answer is no, despite the difficulties that possible incommensurability brings.

Seeing a lack of agreement in educational studies about what education is as a problem to be solved or explored, can be made positive. Many may disagree with me that educational studies tends to foreclose against incommensurable difference. They may bemoan the weakness of educational studies with multiple fractures (Condliffe Lagemann, 2002; Labaree, 2006). Yet, as an 'educationist of difference' I find this lack of agreement invigorating. Diversity of educational modality is a sign of strength in the discipline. Problematically for the development of knowledge about alternatives, my work with alternatives is currently done against the general tide. It is difficult to get it accepted on what one could call its own *other* terms. To be heard at all, I have had to comply to a certain extent to epistemologies that do not match the practices I research. When I do not comply, it can be a fight.

The terrain of otherwise education research is presently viewed almost as irrelevant to the *main* concerns of education departments and as an unusual, interesting perhaps, but really very marginal matter; as a 'novelty'. This is for me, at least, not truth but a sign of a certain repression – part of educationism – that deserves attention for its innocuous effects on education for all, including throughout the life course. We do not tell a black person or a woman that they are marginal because they are in a (constructed) minority, or act towards them as if they were less valuable because of the colour of their skin or their gender. If we do, this is racism and sexism. Something is happening of this kind in education.

If education is acting in this way of resting in its hegemony, the rise of technology has the ability, at least, to challenge an old fashioned educational mentality of one terrain. A sense of education that seems to negate, exclude and ignore alternatives to schooling is unfit for the twenty-first century. Visions of the future with technology are unthinkingly incorporated by adults into what Facer calls a 'chronological imperialism' (2012) but Facer indicates that *this will not do* as an attitude. It fails to accept alternative visions (in her presentation these visions come from the voice of children in schooling). That imperialism will not do *because* of technology is heartening. The repression I currently notice of dismissing alternatives as interesting but not really important in educational studies will then crumble. This will happen through the impactful rise of technology on children's terms of the 'to come ...' (see Lees and Peim, 2013).

Technology is the force that will dissolve this imperialism by virtue, at least, of its mechanistic effects. We won't be able to value the old 'practice' of education because we will practise through new technological tools which ignore old ways of thinking, old institutional modelling, old forms of hierarchies in relationships, old practices of learning. The increasing impact of technology is unstoppable. A concern lies perhaps now in the deep-seated formative 'ways' of technology and its hidden codes, rather than primarily the ways of education (Smedts, 2008; Edwards and Carmichael, 2012).

Arguments for a wider terrain in educational studies are merely a precursor to this inevitable dissolution of the old and increasingly irrelevant; whether we like it or not education is about to change fundamentally. What currently renders alternatives irrelevant will suffer the fate of its own arrogance turned against it, because of nanochips, graphene and radio waves. I have not even mentioned ecological impacts from climate change. With time, this too may create a strong challenge to a non-paradigmatic education-as-schooling.

In this book I point to 'mechanics' of discovery of other educational possibilities from a foreclosed and enframed educational imaginary. Kuhn's framework is deemed to be useful to better understand the movements that discovery makes, and the effects on education as structurally paradigmatic that it illumines. Foucault's care of the self highlights the transformative impacts of EHE as discovery and as practice. Other theoretical perspectives such as 'mu' negations for positive gains of what is liminal are evoked and Hirschman's 'exit' explains much about EHE discovery enthusiasm. I hope a philosophically inclined discussion can be seen as contributing to stimulating deeper and continuing understanding of the rich and significant offering that EHE presents to education and its study.

Kevin Flint and Nick Peim, amongst others, are correct to identify a foreclosure in thinking whereby education develops globally into an enframing technology (Flint and Peim, 2012). What I add to this with the arguments of this book is a further point. The foreclosure noticed is around a singular landscape which involves schooling at its core. This squeezes out educational difference and denies in theory the possibility of what is offered here as a paradigmatic landscape at the structural level of modalities – varying worlds of theory and practice; education without schools and the happy discovery of this possibility. The fact of the diversity of various worlds *which exist* stops foreclosures but we need a moment of discovery that realises this opportunity. Paradigm wars are healthy. All we need are the concepts to fight with.

Appendix

The study

The research investigated the moment of discovery of educational alternatives and in particular contemporary discovery of elective home education (EHE) by parents and other adults in England. The data was set within, and highlighted also, an empirical and theoretical context for this discovery. The study was a PhD project conducted between 2007–2010 with empirical research being done mainly in 2009, via interviews and a street survey.

Interviews

In total the semi-structured interviews numbered 29, with varying degrees of length and number of recorded comments. The duration of the interviews ranged from a few minutes to over three hours, dependent on the serendipitous and practical circumstances of the interaction. Most of the people interviewed were home educating parents or parents considering home educating pre-school age children. Four of the 29 participants were associated with university research, at various levels, concerning EHE and also thorough-going democratic education and were either not home educators or not parents. This category of 29 subjects interviewed were those who were *already aware* of the practice and philosophies of EHE and/or an educational alternatives from a theoretical point of view, or were parents already engaging their children in EHE, intending to do so or thinking about it. The subjects were asked to talk about how they discovered EHE (or other alternatives to mainstream schooling) as a possibility and what that did to them 'internally': to their lives and particularly their sense of self. Participants were asked to describe the effect of the discovery of alternative educational possibilities on their sense of being and self as a philosophical experience of the everyday and to focus in particular on the exact moment they made this discovery.

The street survey

The semi-structured interviews have been triangulated on several points by the street survey data, which has provided evidence that some of the comments made in the interviews are common experiences to be found also 'on the average street'. These interactions usually lasted between (approximately) two minutes to ten minutes. Each interaction was unique to the background of the participant but common themes emerged. In total, 90 people in total were surveyed. These people, met by chance, varied widely in age and ranged from young people of 16 years and above, to pensioners. Survey sheets, with identical boxes for each participant's responses for the researcher to fill in, were used. These captured impressionistic features of the individuals, although no pointed questions about their personal self or circumstances were asked. The street surveys were brief interventions – or mini-interviews – carried out on the streets of towns in the West and East Midlands, or whilst travelling around the UK on public transport.

The interventions were conducted always by starting with the same question: 'Did you know that children don't have to go to school?' This was used as an ice-breaker question in a sense. The question was chosen because, although it is strictly speaking accurate in terms of the law, it captures, in being asked, the assumptions and foreclosed opinions about education that conflate it with school attendance. The use of this question as an ice-breaker was considered a success. It allowed the participants to display their level of conscientisation about education as open to various possibilities. It also enabled conversations as 'openers' between researcher and participant to emerge, often out of initial surprise at the question. Following from a brief answer or discussion in response to this question, further questions were asked.

Ethics

BERA ethical guidelines (BERA, 2004) were followed in the conduct of both the interviews and the street surveys and the project were passed by the ethical framework for research in the School of Education at the University of Birmingham. Further details of the methodology and ethics of this empirical research can be found in the original study publication here: http://etheses.bham.ac.uk/1570/1/Lees11PhD.pdf.

References

Adams, R. and Shepherd, J. (2013) 'Michael Gove proposes longer school day and shorter holidays', *The Guardian*, 18 April.

Adenekan, S. (2007) 'The great giveaway', *The Guardian*, 17 January.

Agamben, G. (2002) 'What is a paradigm?' Lecture at European Graduate School: available at: http://www.egs.edu/faculty/giorgio-agamben/articles/what-is-a-paradigm/.

Agamben, G. (2009) *The signature of all things: On method*, New York, Zone Books.

Alexander, H.A. (2006) 'A view from somewhere: explaining the paradigms of educational research', *Journal of Philosophy of Education*, vol 40, no 2, pp 202-221.

Andreotti, V. and de Souza, L. (2008) 'Translating theory into practice and walking minefields: lessons from the project "Through Other Eyes"', *International Journal of Development Education and Global Learning*, vol 1, no 1, pp 23–36.

Apple, M.W. (2000a) 'Away with all teachers: the cultural politics of home schooling', *International Studies in Sociology of Education*, vol 10, pp 61–80.

Apple, M.W. (2000b) 'The cultural politics of home schooling', *Peabody Journal of Education*, vol 75, no 1 and 2, pp 256–71.

Apple, M.W. (2007) 'Who needs teacher education? Gender, technology, and the work of home schooling.' *Teacher Education Quarterly*, vol 34 no 2, pp 111-30.

Arai, A.B. (1999) 'Homeschooling and the redefinition of citizenship', *Education Policy Analysis Archives*, vol 7, no 27.

Arai, A.B. (2000). 'Reasons for home schooling in Canada.' *Canadian Journal of Education*, vol 25, no 3, pp 204–217.

Argument, B. (2007) 'School's out!' *Teesside Evening Gazette*, 27 February.

Atkinson, M., Martin, K., Downing, D., Harland, J., Kendall, S. and White, R. (2007) *Support for children who are educated at home*, Slough, NFER.

Auxier, R.E. (2002) 'Foucault, Dewey, and the history of the present', *The Journal of Speculative Philosophy*, vol 16, no 2, pp 75–102.

Badman, G. (2009) *Review of elective home education in England*, London, DCSF.

Ball, J. and Brown, S. (2011) 'Why BlackBerry Messenger was rioters' communication method of choice', *The Guardian*, 7 December.

Ball, S. J. (2007) *Education plc: Understanding private sector participation in public sector education*, Abingdon: Routledge.

Bartscherer, T. and Coover, R. (2011) *Switching codes: Thinking through digital technology in the humanities and the arts*, Chicago: University of Chicago Press.

BBC News online (2007) 'Home teaching truancy scam claim', 30 March, available online at http://news.bbc.co.uk/1/hi/education/6509815.stm.

Belenky, M., Clinchy, B., Goldberger, N. and Tarule, J. (1997) *Women's ways of knowing: The development of self, voice, and mind* (10th Anniversary Edition), New York: Basic Books.

Bennis, D. M. and Graves, I. R. (eds) (2007) *The directory of democratic education*, USA: Alternative Education Resource Organisation.

Bentley, A., Earls, M. and O'Brien, M. J. (2011) *I'll have what she's having: Mapping social behaviour*, Cambridge, MA: The MIT Press.

BERA (British Educational Research Association) (2004) *Revised ethical guidelines for educational research*, Macclesfield: British Educational Research Association.

Bergeron, L. (2009) *For the sake of our children*, Toronto: The Alternate Press.

Bernhauer, J. and Rasmussen, D. (1988) *The final Foucault*, Cambridge, MA: The MIT Press.

Bernstein, G. and Triger, Z. (2010) 'Over-parenting', *UC Davis Law Review*, vol 44, pp 1221–79.

Bernstein, R. (1991) 'Incommensurability and otherness revisited', in E. Deutsch (ed) *Culture and modernity*, Honolulu: University of Hawaii Press.

Besley, T. A. C. (2007) 'Foucault, truth-telling and technologies of the self: confessional practices of the self and schools', in Peters, M. A. and Besley, T. A. C. (eds) *Why Foucault? New directions in educational research*, New York: Peter Lang.

Bhopal, K. and Myers, M. (2009) *A pilot study to investigate reasons for elective home education for gypsy and Traveller children in Hampshire,* Report for Hampshire County Council (Ethnic Minority and Traveller Achievement Service).

Biesta, G. J. J. (1994) 'Education as practical intersubjectivity: towards a critical-pragmatic understanding of education', *Educational Theory*, vol 44, no 3, pp 299–317.

Biesta, G. J. J. (2006) *Beyond learning: Democratic education for a human future*, London, Paradigm Publishers.

Biesta, G. J. J. (2007) 'Why "what works" won't work. Evidence-based practice and the democratic deficit of educational research', *Educational Theory*, vol 57, no 1, pp 1–22.

Biesta, G. J. J. (2010) 'A new logic of emancipation: the methodology of Jacques Rancière', *Educational Theory*, vol 60, no 1, pp 39–59.

Biesta, G. and Osberg, D. (2007) 'Beyond re/presentation: a case for updating the epistemology of schooling', *Interchange*, vol 38, no 1, pp 15–29.

Bird, A. (2000) *Thomas Kuhn*, Princeton, NJ: Princeton University Press.

Blair, A. (2007) 'Three times more children taught at home', *The Times*, 24 February .

Block, A. A. (1997) *I'm 'only' bleeding: Education as the practice of violence against children*, New York: Peter Lang Publishing.

Bloom, A. (2009) 'Racist bullying rife in schools, says poll', *Times Educational Supplement*, 1 June.

Bonk, C. J. (2009) *The world is open: How web technology is revolutionising education*, San Franciso, CA, Jossey-Bass.

Bourdieu, P. and Passeron, J.-C. (1990) *Reproduction in education, society and culture*, London: Sage.

Bowles, S. and Gintis, H. (1976) *Schooling in capitalist America*, London: Routledge and Kegan Paul.

Boyle, D. and Harris, M. (2009) *Discussion Paper. The challenge of co-production: how equal partnerships between professionals and the public are crucial to improving public services. NESTA.* Available at: http://www.nesta.org.uk/library/documents/Co-production-report.pdf.

Bruno-Jofré, R. and Zaldívar, J. I. (2012) 'Ivan Illich's late critique of Deschooling Society: "I was largely barking up the wrong tree"', *Educational Theory*, vol 62, no 5, pp 573–92.

Bunz, M. (2010) 'BBC's education service Janala has delivered 1m lessons in three months', *The Guardian*, 17 February.

Butler, J. (2005) 'What is critique? An essay on Foucault's virtue', in Salih, S. and Butler, J. (eds) *The Judith Butler reader*, Oxford: Blackwell Publishing.

Cameron, B. and Meyer, B. (2006) *Self design – nurturing genius through natural learning*, Boulder, CO: Sentient Publications.

Campbell, M. A. (2005) 'Cyber bullying: an old problem in a new guise?', *Australian Journal of Guidance and Counselling*, vol 15, no1, pp 68–76.

Capra, F. (1975) *The Tao of physics: An exploration of the parallels between modern physics and Eastern mysticism*, Boulder, CO: Shambhala.

Capra, F. (1983) *The turning point: Science, society and the rising culture*, London: Fontana Paperbacks.

Carlen, P., Gleeson, D. and Wardhaugh, J. (1992) *Truancy: The politics of complusory schooling*, Buckingham: Open University Press.

Carnie, F. (2003) *Alternative approaches to education: A guide for parents and teachers*, London: Routledge Falmer.

Carper, J. C. (1992) 'Home schooling, history, and historians: the past as present', *High School Journal*, vol 75, pp 252–7.

Carper, J. C. (2000) 'Pluralism to establishment of dissent: the religious and educational context of home schooling', *Peabody Journal of Education*, vol 75, no 1&2, pp 8–19.

Chapman, J. (2012) 'Cameron warns against "gay witch hunt" after Phillip Schofield ambushes him on live TV with list of alleged Tory child abusers', *Daily Mail*, 8 November.

Chavan, M. (2012) *Speech at plenary session of the World Innovation Summit for Education (WISE) 2012 conference*, Doha, Qatar Foundation.

Chester, S. J. (2003) *Conversion at Corinth*, London: T & T Clark.

Children, Schools and Families Committee (2009) 'The review of elective home education: second report of session 2009–10', London: TSO.

Children, Schools and Families Committee (2010) 'From Baker to Balls: the foundations of the education system: ninth report of session 2009–10', London: TSO.

Chokr, N. N. (2009) *Unlearning or how not to be governed?*, Exeter: Imprint Academic.

Conant, J. B. (1951) *Science and common sense*, New Haven: Yale University Press.

Condliffe Lagemann, E. (2002) *An elusive science: The troubling history of education research*, Chicago: University of Chicago Press.

Conroy, J. (2004) *Betwixt and between: The liminal imagination, education, and democracy*, New York, NY: Peter Lang.

Conroy, J. (2009) *Memorandum submitted by Prof. James C Conroy, Dean: Faculty of Education, University of Glasgow*, Select Committee for Children, Schools and Families, House of Commons.

Conroy, J. (2010) 'The state, parenting, and the populist energies of anxiety', *Educational Theory*, vol 60, no 3, pp 325–40.

Conroy, J., Hulme, M. and Menter, I. (2010) 'Primary curriculum futures' in R. Alexander, C. Doddington, J. Gray, L. Hargreaves and R. Kershner (eds), *The Cambridge Primary Review: Research Surveys*, Abingdon: Routledge.

Copenhagen Futures Institute (2009) *Anarconomy*. Copenhagan: Copenhagen Futures Institute. Available at: http://www.cifs.dk/doc/medlemsrapporter/MR0309UK.pdf (accessed 10 November 2012).

Crick, B. (1998) *Education for citizenship and the teaching of democracy in schools: Final report of the advisory group on citizenship*, London: QCA.

Curry, W. B. (1947) *Education for sanity*, London: Heinemann.

Davies, C. (2013) 'Girl, 14, forced to become pregnant with donor sperm bought by mother', *The Guardian*, 28 April.

Davies, R. (2009) 'The affirmation of ordinary life: curricula structure for home education', British Educational Research Association Conference, Manchester University.

Davis, B. (2008) 'Complexity and education: vital simultaneities', *Educational Philosophy and Theory*, vol 40, no 1, pp 50–65.

DCSF (Department for Children, Schools and Families) (2007) *Elective home education: guidelines for local authorities*, London: Department for Children, Schools and Families.

DCSF (2010) *Statistical First Release: pupil absence in schools in England, including pupil characteristics: 2008/09*, London: Department for Children, Schools and Families.

de Oliveira, V. (2012) 'Education, knowledge and the righting of wrongs' *Other Education*, vol 1, no 1, pp 19–31.

Degérando, M. L. B. (1830) *Self education or the means and art of moral progress*, Boston: Carter and Hendee.

Delandshere, G. (2001) 'Implict theories, unexamined assumptions and the status quo of educational assessment', *Assessment in Education*, vol 8, no 2, pp 113–133.

Deleuze, G. and Guattari, F. (2004) *A thousand plateaus*, London: Continuum.

Dewey, J. (1960) *A Common Faith*, New Haven, Yale University Press.

Dewey, J. (1964) 'Need for a philosophy of education', in R. D. Archambault (ed), *John Dewey on education: Selected writings*, New York: Random House.

DfE (Department for Education) (2012) Press release: 'Big business backs new studio schools', Department for Education, 18 July.

Doll, W. E. (1993) *A post-modern perspective on curriculum*, New York: Teachers College Press.

Donmoyer, R. (1996) 'Editorial. Educational research in an era of paradigm proliferation: what's a journal editor to do?', *Educational Researcher*, vol 25, no 2, pp 19–25.

Dowty, T. (2000) *Free range education: How home education works*, Stroud: Hawthorn Press.

D'Marea Bassett, G. (2008) 'Self reliance in life and in learning' in W. Priesnitz (ed), *Life learning*, Toronto: The Alternate Press.

Earl, C. (2006) 'What is effective pedagogy when informally educating electively home-educated children?'. Available at http://www.education-otherwise.org/ResearchIndex.htm

Ecclestone, K. and Hayes, D. (2009) *The dangerous rise of therapeutic education*, Abingdon: Routledge.

Eddis, S. (2007) *A comparative study of attitudes towards home education, held by state officials and home educators in England and Wales and in Florida, USA*, PhD, University of Surrey.

Edwards, R. and Carmichael, P. (2012) 'Secret codes: the hidden curriculum of semantic web technologies', *Discourse: Studies in the cultural politics of education*, vol 33, no 4, pp 575–90.

Elliott, A. (2007) *Concepts of the self*, London: Polity.

Facer, K. (2012) 'Taking the 21st century seriously: young people, education and socio-technical futures', *Oxford Review of Education*, vol 38, no 1, pp 97–113.

Farrell, M. (2012) 'Is home education a human right?', *Global Home Education Conference (GHEC)*, Berlin.

Fielding, M. (2005) 'Alex Bloom, pioneer of radical state education', *FORUM*, vol 47, no 2, pp 119–34.

Fielding, M. (2009) 'Education, identity and the possibility of democratic public space in schools', in ESRC Seminar Series (ed), *The educational and social impact of new technologies on young people in Britain, 'Digital identities: tracing the implications for learners and learning'*, London: London School of Economics.

Fielding, M. (2013) 'Whole School Meetings and the development of radical democratic community', *Studies in Philosophy and Education*, vol 32, no 2, pp 123–40.

Fielding, M. and Moss, P. (2011) *Radical education and the common school: a democratic alternative*, London: Routledge.

Fine, M. (1987) 'Silencing in public schools', *Language Arts*, vol 64, no 2, pp 157–74.

Fleck, L. (1935) *Entstehung and Entwicklung einer Wissenschaftlichen Tatsache, Einfuhrung in die Lehre vom Denkstil und Denkkollektiv*, Basel: Benno Schwabe.

Flint, K.J. and Peim, N. (2012) *Rethinking the education improvement agenda: a critical philosophical approach*, London: Continuum.

Fortune-Wood, M. (2007) *Can't go won't go: An alternative approach to school refusal*, Blaenau Ffestiniog: Cinnamon Press.

Foucault, M. (1977) *Discipline and punish*, London: Penguin.

Foucault, M. (1983a) 'The culture of the self', audiofiles 1, 2 and 3. Berkeley. Available at http://dpg.lib.berkeley.edu/webdb/mrc/search_vod?keyword=foucault

Foucault, M. (1983b) 'On the genealogy of ethics: an overview of work in progress' in P. Rabinow (ed), *Michel Foucault ethics – essential works of Foucault 1954–1984 Volume 1*, London: Penguin.

Foucault, M. (1986) *The care of the self – the history of sexuality, Vol 3*, London: Penguin.

Foucault, M. (1988a) 'The concern for truth' in L. D. Kritzman (ed), *Michel Foucault: Politics, philosophy, culture – interviews and other writings 1977–1984*, New York and London: Routledge.

Foucault, M. (1988b) 'The ethic of care for the self as a practice of freedom', in J. Bernauer and D. Rasmussen (eds), *The final Foucault*, Cambridge, MA: MIT Press.

Foucault, M. (1988c) 'Technologies of the self', in L. H. Martin, H. Gutman and P. H. Hutton (eds), *Technologies of the self: A seminar with Michel Foucault*, London: Tavistock Publications.

Foucault, M. (1991) 'What is enlightenment?', in P. Rabinow (ed), *The Foucault reader*, Harmonsworth: Penguin.

Foucault, M. (1993) 'About the beginning of the hermeneutics of the self: two lectures at Dartmouth', *Political Theory*, vol 21, no 2, pp 198–227.

Foucault, M. (2000) 'Sexuality and solitude', in P. Rabinow (ed), *Michel Foucault ethics – essential works of Foucault 1954–1984, Vol 1*, London: Penguin.

Foucault, M. (2001) *Fearless speech*, Los Angeles: Semiotext.

Foucault, M. (2002) *The order of things*, Abingdon, Oxon: Routledge.

Foucault, M. (2004) *Abnormal: Lectures at the College de France, 1974–1975*, New York: Picador.

Foucault, M. (2005) *The hermeneutics of the subject: Lectures at the College de France 1981-1982*, New York: Picador

Frean, A. (2009) 'Home education "can be cover for abuse and forced marriage"', *The Times*, 20 January.

Frean, A. (2010) 'Exiled: the parents who dared to teach at home', *The Times*, 24 March.

Freire, P. (1996) *Pedagogy of the oppressed*, London: Penguin.

Friedrich, D., Jaastad, B. and Popkewitz, T. S. (2010) 'Democratic education: An (im)possibility that yet remains to come', *Educational Philosophy and Theory*, vol 42, no 5–6, pp 571–87.

Gaither, M. (2008) *Homeschool: An American history*, New York: Palgrave MacMillan.

George, M. (2008) *The 7 Aha!s of highly enlightened souls*, Ropley: O Books.

Giddens, A. (2000) *Runaway world*, London: Routledge.

Glanzer, P. (2008) 'Rethinking the boundaries and burdens of parental authority over education: a response to Rob Reich's case study of homeschooling', *Educational Theory*, vol 58, no 1, pp 1–16.

Glendinning, L. (2008) 'Khyra Ishaq: "starved" girl's mother appears in court', *The Guardian*, 28 May.

Glenn, C. (2004) *Unspoken: A rhetoric of silence*, Carbondale: Southern Illinois Press.

Glover, D., Gough, G., Johnson, M. and Cartwright, N. (2000) 'Bullying in 25 secondary schools: incidence, impact and intervention', *Educational Research*, vol 42, no 2, pp 141–156.

Goodman, A. and Gregg, P. (2010) 'Poorer children's educational attainment: how important are attitudes and behaviour?'. Available at http://www.jrf.org.uk/publications/educational-attainment-poor-children

Goodsman, D. (1992) *Summerhill: theory and practice*, Norwich, Unpublished PhD thesis, University of East Anglia.

Gould, M. (2008) 'Liberation theory' (Interview: Simon Duffy), *The Guardian*, 30 January.

Gribble, D. (2001) *Worlds apart*, London: Libertarian Education.

Gribble, D. (2012) 'Who asks the questions?', *Other Education*, vol 1, no 1, pp 141–51.

Guba, E. C. (1990) 'The alternative paradigm dialog' in E. C. (ed), *The paradigm dialog*, Newbury Park, CA: Sage.

Gutherson, P. and Mountford-Lees, J. (2011) 'New models for organising education: "flexi-schooling" – how one school does it well', Reading: CfBT.

Hacking, I. (1996) 'Normal people' in D. R. Olson and N. Torrance (eds), *Modes of thought: Explorations in culture and cognition*, Cambridge: Cambridge University Press.

Harber, C. (2004) *Schooling as violence: How schools harm pupils and societies*, London: Routledge Falmer.

Harber, C. (2008) 'Perpetrating disaffection: schooling as an international problem', *Educational Studies*, vol 34, no 5, pp 457–67.

Harber, C. (2009a) 'Revolution, what revolution?': contextual issues in citizenship education in schools in England', *Citizenship, Social and Economics Education*, vol 8, no 2, pp 42–53.

Harber, C. (2009b) *Toxic schooling: How schools became worse*, Nottingham: Educational Heretics Press.

Harber, C. and Mncube, V. (2012) 'Democracy, education and development: theory and reality', *Other Education*, vol 1, no 1, pp 104–20.

Harber, C., and Mncube, V. (2013) *Education, democracy and development – does education contribute to democratisation in developing countries?*, Oxford: Symposium Books.

Harkin, J. (2008) 'Strictly asking for it', *The Guardian*, 20 November.

Harris, S. (2007) 'Internet schools: the school on a sofa', *The Independent*, 28 October.

Harrison, I. (2010) *Iris's story*, unpublished book manuscript.

Hart, T. (2004) 'Opening the contemplative mind in the classroom', *Journal of Transformative Education*, vol 2, no 1, pp 28–46.

Hase, S. and Kenyon, C. (2000) 'From andragogy to heutagogy', *Ultibase*. Available at http://pandora.nla.gov.au/nph-wb/20010220130000/http://ultibase.rmit.edu.au/Articles/dec00/hase2.htm, December.

Hase, S. and Kenyon, C. (2007) 'Heutagogy: a child of complexity theory', *Complicity: an International Journal of Complexity and Education*, vol 4, no 1, pp 111–18.

Healy, P. (2001) 'A "limit attitude": Foucault, autonomy, critique', *History of the Human Sciences*, vol 14, no 1, pp 49–68.

HEAS (Home Education Advisory Service) to House of Commons Education Committee (2012) Written evidence, 'Support for Home Education', *Fifth Report of Session 2012–13: Volume I – Report, together with formal minutes, oral and written evidence*, London: TSO.

Henry, S. E. (2013) 'Bodies at home and at school: toward a theory of embodied social class status', *Educational Theory*, vol 63, no 1, pp 1–16.

Hern, M. (2003) *Field day – Getting society out of school*, Vancouver: New Star Books.

Hern, M. (ed) (2008) *Everywhere all the time: A new deschooling reader*, Oakland, CA: A K Press.

Hirschman, A. O. (1970) *Exit, voice, and loyalty*, Cambridge, MA: Harvard University Press.

Holt, J. (1977) *Instead of education*, Harmondsworth: Penguin.

Holt, J. (2003) *Teach your own*, Cambridge, MA: Perseus Publishing.

House of Commons Education Committee (2012) 'Support for Home Education', *Fifth Report of Session 2012–13: Volume I – Report, together with formal minutes, oral and written evidence*, London: TSO.

House of Commons Education Committee (2013) *Support for Home Education: Government Response to the Committee's Fifth Report of Session 2012–13*, London: TSO.

Hyland, T. (2011) *Mindfulness and learning: Celebrating the affective dimension of education*, Dordrecht: Springer.

James, S. (2012) *Sex, race and class – The perspective of winning: A selection of writings 1952–2011*, Oakland, CA: PM Press.

James, S. and Dalla Costa, M. (1972) *The power of women and the subversion of the community*, Bristol: Falling Wall Press.

Jarrett, T. and Bolton, P. (2012) 'School funding, including the pupil premium' published 26 July. Standard notes SN04581.

Kalamaras, G. (1994) *Reclaiming the Tacit Dimension*, New York: State University of New York Press.

Kincheloe, J. L. (2001) 'Describing the bricolage: conceptualizing a new rigor in qualitative research', *Qualitative Inquiry*, vol 7, no 6, pp 679–92.

Knowles, J. G., Marlow, S. E. and Muchmore, J. A. (1992) 'From pedagogy to ideology: origins and phases of home education in the United States, 1970–1990. *American Journal of Education*', vol 100, no 2, pp 195–235.

Knowles, M. (1975) *Self-directed learning: A guide for students and teachers*, New Jersey: Prentice Hall.

Knowles, M. S., Holton, E. F. and Swanson, R. A. (2005) *The adult learner: The definitive classic in adult education and human resource development*, Burlington, MA: Elsevier.

Knox, H. (2008) 'Homeschooling as a single parent', in M. Hern (ed), *Everywhere all the time: A new deschooling reader*, Oakland, CA: A K Press.

Kuhn, T. S. (1962) *The structure of scientific revolutions*, Chicago: Chicago University Press.

Kuhn, T. S. (2000a) 'Commensurability, comparability, communicability', in J. Conant and Haugeland, J. (eds), *The road since structure: Philosophical essays, 1970–1993, with an Autobiographical Interview*, Chicago: University of Chicago Press.

Kuhn, T. S. (2000b) 'What are scientific revolutions?', in J. Conant and J. Haugeland (eds), *The road since structure: Philosophical essays, 1970–1993, with an autobiographical interview*, Chicago: Chicago University Press.

Kunzman, R. (2009) *Write these laws on your children: Inside the world of conservative Christian homeschooling*, Boston, MA: Beacon Press.

Kunzman, R. (2012) 'Education, schooling, and children's rights: the complexity of homeschooling', *Educational Theory*, vol 62, no 1, pp 75–89.

Kunzman, R. and Gaither, M. (2013) 'Homeschooling: A comprehensive survey of the research', *Other Education*, vol 2, no 1, pp 4–59.

Labaree, D. F. (2006) *The trouble with ed schools*, New Haven and London: Yale University Press.

Lane, H. (1928) *Talks to parents and teachers*, London: George Allen and Unwin Ltd.

Lawson, M. (2008) 'The screaming Lord Sutch of the dancefloor', *The Guardian*, 20 November.

Leadbetter, C. (2012) *Innovation in education: Lesson from pioneers around the world*, Doha: Bloomsbury Qatar Foundation Publishing.

Leadbetter, C. and Wong, A. (2010) *Learning from the extremes*, San Jose, CA: Cisco.

Leander, K.M. (2002) 'Silencing in classroom interaction: Producing and relating social spaces', *Discourse Processes*, vol 34, no 2, pp 193–235.

Lees, H. (2008) 'The democratic School Meeting and Foucault's "Care of the self": Technologies of the self in practice for purpose' in C. Corcoran, N. MacNab, E. Lucas-Gardiner and W. Milner (eds), *School of Education Student Conference*, Birmingham: University of Birmingham School of Education.

Lees, H.E. (2011a) 'The Gateless Gate of home education discovery: what happens to the self of adults upon discovery of the possibility and possibilities of an educational alternative?', PhD, *Department of Education*. Birmingham: University of Birmingham.

Lees, H.E. (2011b) 'Philosophy of education at the edge of the world: the concept of education revisited ...', *Philosophy of Education Great Britain Conference, Proceedings*, Philosophy of Education Society Great Britain.

Lees, H.E. (2011c) 'Transformed by discovery at the modality level: Schooling as one educational paradigm and elective home education as another ...', *PESGB Conference Symposium on Women in Philosophy of Education*. New College, Oxford.

Lees, H.E. (2012) 'The tyrannical principle of the educational sign', *British Educational Research Association annual conference, Manchester University*.

Lees, H.E. (2013a) 'Alternative education in Scotland', in W. Humes and T. Bryce (eds), *Scottish Education 4th Edition*, Edinburgh: University of Edinburgh Press.

Lees, H.E. (2013b) 'Is the idea of compulsory schooling ridiculous?', in M. Papastephanou (ed), *Philosophical Persepectives on Compulsory Education*, Dortrecht: Springer.

Lees, H.E. and Peim, N. (2013) 'Prelude to the school to come ...', Introduction to the special issue, *Studies in Philosophy and Education*, vol 32, no 2, pp 113–22.

Levi-Strauss, C. (1966) *The savage mind*, Chicago: The University of Chicago Press.

Llewellyn, G. (ed) (1993) *Real lives: Eleven teenagers who don't go to school*, Eugene, OR: Lowry House.

Llewellyn, G. (1998) *The teenage liberation handbook: How to quit school and get a real life and education*, Eugene: OR, Lowry House.

Lloyd, C.B. and Mensch, B.S. (2006) 'Marriage and childbirth as factors in school exit: an analysis of DHS data from sub-Saharan Africa', *Policy Research Division Working Papers*, New York: Population Council.

Lloyd, N. (2012) 'New primary school plans scrapped in Coventry after academies row', *The Guardian*, 16 October.

Lyotard, J.-F. (1984) *The postmodern condition: A report on knowledge*, Manchester: Manchester University Press.

Macfarlane, A.H. (2012) '"Other" education down-under: indigenising the discipline for psychologists and specialist educators', *Other Education*, vol 1, no 1, pp 205–25.

Maddern, K. (2009) 'Minister urges headteachers to tackle special needs bullying and exclusions', *Times Educational Supplement*, 20 February.

Marr, N. and Field, T. (2001) *Bullycide: Death at playtime*, Didcot: Success Unlimited.

Marsh, P., Rosser, E. and Harre, R. (1978) *The rules of disorder*, London: Routledge Keagan Paul.

Masterman, M. (ed) (1970) *The nature of a paradigm*, Cambridge: Cambridge University Press.

McAvoy, P. (2012) '"There are no housewives on Star Trek": a reexamination of exit rights for the children of insular fundamentalist parents', *Educational Theory*, vol 62, no 5, pp 535–52.

McCulloch, G. (1998) *Failing the ordinary child? The theory and practice of working-class secondary education*, Buckingham: Open University Press.

McKee, A. (2002) *Homeschooling our children unschooling ourselves*, Madison: Bittersweet House.

McKie, R. (2008) 'How the beat of our feet can generate power', *The Observer*, 30 November.

McLaughlin, T. H. (2000) 'Citizenship education in England: the Crick report and beyond', *Journal of Philosophy of Education*, vol 34, no 4, pp 541–70.

Medlin, R.G. (2000) 'Home schooling and the question of socialization', *Peabody Journal of Education*, vol 75, no 1&2, pp 107–23.

Mehta, J. (2013) 'How paradigms create politics: the Transformation of American educational policy, 1980–2001', *American Educational Research Journal*, vol 50, no 2, pp 285–324.

Meighan, R. (1984) 'Political consciousness and home-based education', *Educational Review*, vol 36, no 2, pp 165–73.

Meighan, R. (ed) (1992) *Learning from home-based education*, Nottingham: Education Now Books.

Meighan, R. (1995) 'Home-based education effectiveness research and some of its implications.' *Educational Review* vol 47, no 3, pp 275-287.

Meighan, R. (2004) *Damage limitation: Trying to reduce the harm schools do to children*, Nottingham: Educational Heretics Press.

Meighan, R. (2005) *Comparing learning systems: The good, the bad, the ugly, and the counter-productive*, Nottingham: Educational Heretics Press.

Merrills, J.G. (1995) *The development of international law by the European Court of Human Rights*, Manchester, Manchester University Press.

Merry, M. S. and Howell, C. (2009) 'Can intimacy justify home education?', *Theory and Research in Education*, vol 7, no 3, pp 363–81.

Mey, M. D. (1992) *The cognitive paradigm: An integrated understanding of scientific development*, Chicago: The University of Chicago Press.

Miller, R. (2008) *The self-organising revolution*, Brandon: Psychology Press/Holistic Education Press.

Mintz, J. and Ricci, C. (Eds.) (2010) *Turning points: 27 visionaries in education tell their own stories*, USA: Alternative Education Resource Organisation.

Mitra, S., Dangwal, R., S.Chatterjee, Jha, S., Bisht, R. and Kapur, P. (2005) 'Acquisition of computer literacy on shared public computers: children and the "hole in the wall"', *Australasian Journal of Educational Technology*, vol 21, no 3, pp 407–26.

Moore, R.S. and Moore, D. (1988) *Home school burnout: What it is, what causes it, and how to overcome it*, Brentwood, TN: Wolgemuth and Hyatt Pub.

Moore, T. (2010) 'Give me your tired, your poor, your homeschoolers', *Time Magazine*, 1 March.

Morton, R. (2010a) 'Home education: constructions of choice', *International Electronic Journal of Elementary Education*, vol 3, no 1, pp 45–56.

Morton, R. (2010b) 'Walking the line: home education as a fine balance between parental fulfilment and hard labour', *British Sociological Conference*, Glasgow.

nef (2008) *Co-production*. London: New Economics Foundation.

Neill, A.S. (1936) *Is Scotland educated?*, London: Routledge.

Neill, A.S. (1966) *Freedom: Not license!*, New York: Hart Publishing Company, Inc.

Neill, A.S. (1968) *Summerhill*, Harmondsworth: Penguin.

Neuman, A. and Avriam, A. (2003) Homeschooling as a fundamental change in lifestyle, *Evaluation and Research in Education*, vol 17, no 2–3, pp 132–43.

New, R.S. and Cochrane, M. (eds) (2007) *Early childhood education (four volumes): An international encyclopaedia*, Westport, CT: Praeger Publishing.

Nicholson, F. (2011) 'How many home educated children?' FOI England.

Nisbett, R.E. (2005) *The geography of thought*, London: Nicholas Brealey Publishing.

Oliver, C. and Kandappa, M. (2003) *Tackling bullying: Listening to the views of children and young people*, London: DfES and ChildLine.

Olsen, C. (2000) *Zen and the art of postmodern philosophy – two paths of liberation from the representational mode of thinking*, Albany: State University of New York Press.

Olson, K. (2009) *Wounded by school: Recapturing the joy in learning and standing up to old school culture*, New York: Teachers College Press.

Olssen, M. (2007) 'Invoking democracy: Foucault's conception (with insights from Hobbes)', in M.A. Peters and T.A.C. Besley (eds), *Why Foucault? New directions in educational research*, New York: Peter Lang.

Osberg, D., Biesta, G. and Cilliers, P. (2008) 'From representation to emergence: complexity's challenge to the epistemology of schooling', *Educational Philosophy and Theory*, vol 40, no 1, pp 213–27.

Osberg, D. and Biesta, G.J.J. (2007) 'Beyond presence: epistemological and pedagogical implications of "strong" emergence, *Interchange*, vol 38, no 1, pp 31–51.

Osler, A. (2006) 'Excluded girls: interpersonal, institutional and structural violence in schooling', *Gender and Education*, vol 18, no 6, pp 571–89.

Papay, J.P., Murnane, R.J. and Willett, J.B. (2008) 'The Consequences of high school exit examinations for struggling low-income urban students: evidence from Massachusetts', *NBER Working Paper Series*, Cambridge, MA: National Bureau of Economic Research.

Parr, C. (2013) 'How was it? The UK's first Coursera MOOCs assessed', *Times Higher Education*, 18 April.

Parsons, S. and Lewis, A. (2010) 'The home-education of children with special needs or disabilities in the UK: views of parents from an online survey', *International Journal of Inclusive Education*, vol 14, no 1, pp 67–86.

Pattison, H. (2013) 'Interview with Jonas Himmelstrand', *Other Education*, vol 2, no 1, pp 67–74.

Peim, N. (2013) 'Education, schooling, Derrida's Marx and democracy: some fundamental questions', *Studies in Philosophy and Education*, vol 32, no 2, pp 171–87.

Peim, N. and Flint, K.J. (2009) 'Testing times: Questions concerning assessment for school improvement', *Educational Philosophy and Theory*, vol 41, no 3, pp 342–61.

Pendlebury, S. (2005) 'Feminism, epistemology and education', in W. Carr (ed), *The Routledge Falmer reader in philosophy of education*, Abingdon: Routledge.

Peters, R.S. (1973) 'Introduction', in R. S. Peters (ed), *The philosophy of education*, Oxford: Oxford University Press.

Phillips, S. (2004) 'Home-schoolers on the rise', *Times Educational Supplement*, 13 August.

Pilkington, C.L. and Piersel, W.C. (1991) 'School phobia – a critical analysis of the separation anxiety theory and an alternative conceptualization', *Psychology in the Schools*, vol 28, no 4, pp 290–303.

Preston, J. (2008) *Kuhn's 'The structure of scientific revolutions'*, London, Continuum.

Princiotta, D., and Bielick, S. (2006) *Homeschooling in the United States: 2003 statistical analysis report (NCES 2006-042)*, Washington, DC: US Department of Education National Center for Educational Statistics.

Puckett, W. (2011) 'What makes 38 Degrees a powerful voice for change?', *The Guardian*, 8 April.

Radford, J. (2010) Serious Case Review: Case No 14 (Khyra Ishaq death), Birmingham, Birmingham Safeguarding Children Board.

Reay, D. (2001) 'Finding or losing yourself? Working-class relationships to education', *Journal of Education Policy*, vol 16, no 4, pp 333–46.

Reich, R. (2005) 'Why home schooling should be regulated' in B. S. Cooper (ed), *Home schooling in full view: A reader*, Charlotte, NC: Information Age Publishing.

Reimer, F. (2010) 'School attendance as a civic duty v. home education as a human right', *International Electronic Journal of Elementary Education*, vol 3, no 1, pp 5–15.

Reps, P. (ed) (2000) *Zen flesh Zen bones: A collection of Zen and pre-Zen writings*, London: Penguin.

Revill, J. (2007) 'Revolution in home care for old people', *The Observer*, 9 December.

Roberts, P. (2012) 'Bridging East and West – or, a bridge too far? Paulo Freire and the Tao Te Ching', *Educational Philosophy and Theory*, vol 44, no 9, pp 942–58.

Robinson, K. (2010) 'Bring on the learning revolution', TED Lectures.

Rogers, L. (2005) 'Number of children taught at home soars', *The Sunday Times*, 26 June.

Röhrs, H. (1995) 'Internationalism in progressive education and intitial steps towards a world education movement', in H. Röhrs and V. Lenhart (ed), *Progressive education across the continents*, Frankfurt am Main: Peter Lang.

Röhrs, H. and Lenhart, V. (eds) (1995) *Progressive education across the continents*, Frankfurt am Main: Peter Lang.

Roland Martin, J. (2003) 'Feminism: The missing women', in R. Curren (ed), *A companion to the philosophy of education*, Oxford: Blackwell.

Roland Martin, J. (2011) *Education reconfigured: Culture, encounter, and change*, London: Routledge.

Rothermel, P. (2002) 'Home-education: Rationales, practices and outcomes', PhD Thesis, University of Durham.

Rothermel, P. (2003) 'Can we classify motives for home education?', *Evaluation and Research in Education*, vol 17, no 2–3, pp 74–89.

Rothermel, P. (2010) 'Home education: practising without prejudice?', *Every Child Journal*, vol 1, no 5, pp 48–53.

Routledge, P. (2010) 'Pictures of Kyra (sic) Ishaq are haunting', *The Mirror*, 30 July.

Safran, L. (2008) 'Exploring identity change and communities of practice among long term home educating parents', PhD Thesis, *Centre for Research in Education and Educational Technology (CREET)*, Milton Keynes: The Open University.

Safran, L. (2010) 'Legitimate peripheral participation and home education', *Teaching and Teacher Education*, vol 26, no 1, pp 107–12.

Safran, L. (2012) 'Home education: the power of trust', *Other Education*, vol 1, no 1, pp 32–45.

Sample, I. (2007) 'The future of design? Voters pick the next must-have on the net', *The Guardian*, 24 November.

Schoolhouse (2010) Press Release: 'Scottish Government upholds freedom of choice in education'. Available at: http://www.schoolhouse.org.uk/home-ed-in-the-news/scottish-government-upholds-freedom-of-choice-in-education

Scottish Government (2007) *Home Education Guidance*, Edinburgh: Scottish Government.

Sheffer, S. (1995) *A sense of self – listening to home schooled adolescent girls*, Portsmouth, New Hampshire: Boynton/Cook Publishers.

Shepherd, J. (2010a) 'Khyra Ishaq tragedy: ministers urged to tighten law on home education', *The Guardian*, 27 July.

Shepherd, J. (2010b) 'Truancy rate at record high', *The Guardian*, 25 March.

Skidelsky, R. (1969) *English progressive schools*, Harmondsworth: Penguin.

Smedts, G. (2008) 'Parenting in a technological age', *Ethics and Education*, vol 3, no 2, pp 121–34.

Smith, F. (1998) *The book of learning and forgetting*, New York: Teachers College Press.

Smith, R. (2010) 'Total parenting', *Educational Theory*, vol 60, no 3, pp 357–69.

Spender, D. (1980) *Man made language*, London: Routledge and Kegan Paul.

Spiegler, T. (2003) 'Home education in Germany: an overview of the contemporary situation', *Evaluation and Research in Education*, vol 17, no 2&3, pp 179–90.

Spring, J. (1998) *A primer of libertarian education*, Montreal: Black Rose Books.

Srivastava, P. (ed) (2013) *Low-fee private schooling: Aggravating equity or mitigating disadvatage?* Oxford: Symposium Books.

Staff Writer (2008) '"Lesbian" jibes drive 14-yr-old to suicide', *Metro*, 10 January.

Stafford, B. (2012) 'Bad evidence: the curious case of the government-commissioned review of elective home education in England and how parents exposed its weaknesses', *Evidence & Policy: A Journal of Research, Debate and Practice*, vol 8, no 3, pp 361–81.

Stanford, P. K. (2006) *Exceeding our grasp: Science, history, and the problem of unconceived alternatives*, Oxford: Oxford University Press.

Stevens, M. (2003a) *Kingdom of children: Culture and controversy in the homeschooling movement*, Princeton: Princeton University Press.

Stevens, M. L. (2003b) 'The normalisation of homeschooling in the USA', *Evaluation and Research in Education*, vol 17, no 2–3, pp 90–100.

Stickney, J. (2006) 'Deconstructing discourses about "new paradigms of teaching": a Foucaultian and Wittgensteinian perspective', *Educational Philosophy and Theory*, vol 38, no 3, pp 327–71.

Stronach, I. (2005) 'Progressivism against the audit culture: the continuing case of Summerhill School versus OfSTED', *First International Congress of Qualitative Inquiry*, University of Illinois at Urbana-Champaign.

Stronach, I. (2010) 'Has progressive education a future? The fall and rise of Summerhill School', *British Educational Research Association Annual Conference*, Warwick University.

Stronach, I. and Piper, H. (2008) 'Can liberal education make a comeback? The case of "relational touch" at Summerhill School', *American Educational Research Journal*, vol 45, no 1, pp 6–37.

Sugden, J. (2009) 'Parents protest at Ofsted inspections for children taught at home', *The Times*, 14 September.

Suissa, J. (2006) 'Untangling the mother knot: some thoughts on parents, children and philosophers of education', *Ethics and Education*, vol 1, no 1, pp 65–77.

Suissa, J. (2010) *Anarchism and education – a philosophical exploration*, Oakland, CA: PM Press.

Summerhill School (2000) Press statement issued by Summerhill School in response to the High Court victory against Ofsted, 23 March.

Szakolczai, A. (1994) 'Thinking beyond the East–West divide: Foucault, Patocka, and the care of the self', *Social Research*, vol 61, no 2, pp 297–323.

Thomas, A. (1998) *Educating Children at Home*, London: Cassell.

Thomas, A. (2013) 'Autonomous and informal education under threat: Summerhill, UK, Sudbury Schools in The Netherlands and home education.' *Other Education*, vol 2, no 1, pp 75-77.

Thomas, A. and Pattison, H. (2007) *How children learn at home*, London: Continuum.

Thomas, A. and Pattison, H. (2010) 'Home education: precious, not dangerous', *The Guardian*, 28 July.

Thomas, A. and Pattison, H. (2013) 'Informal home education: philosophical aspirations put into practice', *Studies in Philosophy and Education*, vol 32, no 2, pp 141–54.

Tobin, G.A. and Ybarra, D.R. (2008) *The trouble with textbooks: Distorting history and religion*, Lanham, MD: Lexington Books.

Tomasevski, K. (2003) *Education denied: Costs and remedies*, London: Zed Books.

Tomasevski, K. (2005) 'Has the right to education a future within the united nations? A behind-the-scenes account by the special rapporteur on the right to education 1998–2004', *Human Rights Law Review*, vol , no 25, pp 205–37.

Tooley, J. (2009) *The beautiful tree: A personal journey into how the world's poorest people are educating themselves*, Washington: Cato Institute.

Toulmin, S. (1972) *Human understanding: The collective use and evolution of concepts*, Princeton: Princeton University Press.

Trafford, B. (2003) *School councils, school democracy, school improvement: Why, what, how?*, Leicester: Secondary Heads Association.

Twining, P. (2007). *The Schome NAGTY teen second life pilot final report: A summary of key findings & lessons learnt*, Milton Keynes: The Open University.

Tyack, D. and Cuban, L. (1995) *Tinkering towards utopia: A century of public school reform*, Cambridge, MA: Harvard University Press.

United Nations (1948) *Universal declaration of human rights*, General Assembly of the United Nations.

Vidal, J. (2007) 'She has changed the national perspective about plastic bags in a few months. She should be prime minister', *The Guardian*, 23 November.

Villalba, C.M. (2009) 'Home-based education in Sweden: local variations in forms of regulation', *Theory and Research in Education*, vol 7, no 3, pp 277–96.

Waks, L. (2012) 'Education 2.0: teaching and learning in the information age', *Other Education*, vol 1, no 1, pp 188–204.

Walton, G. (2005) '"Bullying widespread": a critical analyis of research and public discourse on bullying', *Journal of School Violence*, vol 4, no 1, pp 91–118.

Ward, K. (2008) *Augenblick: The concept of the 'decisive moment' in 19th- and 20th-Century Western philosophy*, Aldershot, Hampshire: Ashgate Publishing.

Watts, A. (1974) *Nothingness*, Milbrae, California: Celestial Arts.

Wheeler, B. (2012) 'Home schooling: Why more black US families are trying it', *BBC News Magazine*, 15 March. Available at: http://www.bbc.co.uk/news/magazine-17224662.

Willis, P.E. (1981) *Learning to labour: How working class kids get working class jobs*, New York: Columbia University Press.

Wills, D. (1947) *The Barns experiment*, London: Allen and Unwin.

Wittgenstein, L. (2001) *Tractatus logico-philosophicus*, London: Routledge.

www.applyESL.com (2010) 'Choose the best school for you'. Available at: http://www.applyesl.com/topics/03/?lid=0.

Wray, A. and Thomas, A. (2013) 'School refusal and home education', *Journal of Unschooling and Alternative Learning*, vol 7, no 13, pp 64–85.

Yoneyama, S. (1999) *The Japanese high school: Silence and resistence*, London: Routledge.

Yoneyama, S. (2000) 'Student discourse on tokokyohi (school phobia/refusal) in Japan: burnout or empowerment?', *British Journal of Sociology of Education*, vol 21, no 1, pp 77–94.

Zerubavel, E. (2006) *The elephant in the room: Silence and denial in everyday life*, Oxford: Oxford University Press.

Index

Page references for notes are followed by n